DESTROY THIS TEMPLE

DESTROY THIS TEMPLE

The Voice of Black Power in Britain

Obi Egbuna

BLACK CLASSIC PRESS
Baltimore

Destroy This Temple
The Voice of Black Power in Britain

~Originally Published by Granada Publishing LTD~

Copyright 1971 Obi Egbuna
Introduction copyright by Obi Egbuna Jr. 2022

Published 2022 by Black Classic Press

Library of Congress Control Number: 2020949093

Print book ISBN: 978-1-57478-199-1
E-book ISBN: 978-1-57478-200-4

Printed by BCP Digital Printing (www.bcpdigital.com)
an affiliate company of Black Classic Press Inc.
For a virtual tour of our publishing and printing facility visit:
https://www.c-span.org/video/?441322-2/tour-black-classic-press

Purchase Black Classic Press books from your favorite bookseller
or online at: www.blackclassicbooks.com

For inquiries or to request a list of titles, write:
Black Classic Press
P.O. Box 13414
Baltimore, MD 21203

New Introduction
Obi Egbuna Jr.

WHEN epic books aimed at capturing the direction of African people's genuine resistance are republished, readers are presented with two golden opportunities. The first is the prospect of absorbing the content of previously written material in its original form, as originally intended. The second is the opportunity to learn about both the impact early writers made at that exact historical moment as well as the primary influences that shaped their thinking and actions. Before readers of this republished volume attempt to wrap their heads around the circumstances and developments that led to my father emerging as one of the co-founders of both the Black Panther Party and Black Power Movement in London, let me avail you of the latter opportunity and share some insights about how and why Obi Egbuna Sr. came to England and the US in the first place.

It is well documented that the former colonizers and captors of Africa not only grappled with the idea of letting their colonial subjects and human chattel have access to formal education, but they also engaged in extremely contentious and acrimonious debates about whether that masquerade of compassion might lead to their very demise. Within this polemical milieu, several scholarships, endowments, and foundations were created by and/or named in honor of ruthless individuals the likes of Rhodes, Carnegie, Rockefeller, and so on. Africans at home and abroad, however—whether in Tanzania, the Congo, or Mississippi—can relate to the daily challenges met by those chosen to pursue formal education in the belly of the beast while those left behind remained at the political and economic mercy of foreign juggernauts.

My father's journey represents that traditional yet enduringly offensive narrative of colonial education and immigration highlighting one of the rare occasions when our exploiters opted to display human decency. In his youth, he won a scholarship that made it possible for him to go to England to study, traveling approximately 4,117 miles from Nigeria to pursue and obtain a degree in electrical engineering. Such opportunities were only made available to an extremely minute group of students, but the everyday villagers in the town of Ozubulu celebrated my father's achievement in a manner that would have given outside observers the impression that invading, raping, and plundering our sacred land was perfectly okay—provided they occasionally gave a few individuals a chance at normalcy.

The way it was explained to me during numerous father-son meetings of the minds, *Destroy This Temple* was my father's humble attempt not to commit what one of his favorite writers, Dr. W. E. B. Du Bois, called the "unforgivable sin": when freedom fighters on the frontlines fail to record and chronicle their work. That fatal omission, both believed, served only to open the doors for distant observers or cultural outsiders to contaminate and pollute the narrative. The book's reception demonstrated a heartfelt and honest appreciation for a history of the Black Power Movement and Black Panther Party in London written by a central figure in those two movements, both of which owed their very existences to the climate and atmosphere that produced the Fifth Pan-African Congress in Manchester, England, in 1945.

Eight years before *Destroy This Temple* was released, another of my father's early works, *Wind Versus Polygamy* (1964) was published. That novel was extremely vital for revealing the existence of a new group of continental-born African writers who were ready and able to use creative writing as a vehicle for climbing up the ladder-like process of decolonization. Their works, like those of my father, supported the notion that Africans collectively, throughout the Diaspora, would achieve full cultural and historical reclamation, which would go hand and hand with political power. Two years later, *Wind Versus Polygamy* was transformed into a play and ended up being London's submission to the First World and Arts Festival in Dakar, Senegal, in 1966. Another crucial piece from the catalogue of my father's creative writing during his London years was a play titled *The Anthill* (1965).

The strong Nationalist and Pan-Africanist fervor that peppered the pages of *Destroy This Temple* was again on display in an essay he wrote that was published by PANAF books. That piece, *The Murder of Nigeria* (1968), unambiguously contextualized and condemned the genocidal and neocolonialist nature of the Ibo-Biafran War. It also generated praise from both Shirley Graham Du Bois and Osagyefo Dr. Kwame Nkrumah, which led to an invitation for him to visit Nkrumah in Conakry, Guinea in 1968.

A particular grouping of this collection's readership may be more familiar with other of my father's creative works like *The Emperor of the*

New Introduction

Sea (1974), *The Minister's Daughter* (1975), and *Diary of a Homeless Prodigal* (1976), which represent the broad spectrum of his creative reflections about his return to Nigeria from 1972 to 1976. During that period, he launched the first-ever writers' workshop in modern Nigerian history while simultaneously serving as the director of ECBS Television in Nigeria's East Central State. He also produced a pamphlet called *The ABC of Black Power Thought* (1973), dedicated to the Osagyefo.

Leaving Nigeria for the U.S., my father accepted an invitation to participate in the internationally renowned Iowa Writers Workshop, earning an MFA degree from that program in 1978 based on his thesis, "Author's Diary: Impressions from Three Worlds." In 1980, four of his creative works were published: *Divinity: A Radio Play*, *The Madness of Didi*, *The Rape of Lysistrata*, and *Black Candle for Christmas*. He later attended Howard University, earning a PhD in African Studies in 1986. His dissertation was titled, "The Dialectical Process in Modern African Literature: A Study in the Epistemology of Decolonization."

The reintroduction of *Destroy This Temple* will shatter the myth that Black Power, conceptually, and the Black Panther Party, politically, should only be framed and discussed as part of the amputated narrative of the collective African experience. It further capitates presumptions that these two movements are reserved exclusively for Africans born and raised in North America—as if Mother Africa exists in another part of the solar system!

Among the book's myriad revelations are my father's discussion of how the most Honorable Elijah Muhammad received the two key voices of the 1960s Black Power Movement, Obi Egbuna Sr. and Kwame Ture, at his private residence on the heels of Brother Malcolm's assassination at the hands of the NYPD, FBI, and CIA. Each and every reader of *Destroy This Temple* will come to understand the inseparability of the Black Panther Party from the Black Power Movement, a dynamism that caused paternalistic white liberals in North America and Western Europe countless sleepless nights. The role of Brother Kwame in spreading the truth about both the Party and the Movement will get a well-deserved boost from this book. My father's fondness for Ture and the deep admiration they both had for Dr. Nkrumah are also abundantly perceptible in this volume, which relates the details of my father's arrest after he brought the Osagyefo's pamphlet, *Message to the Black People of Britain*, back to England in its manuscript form.

Destroy This Temple will fuel our young people's eagerness for firsthand accounts of service and sacrifice in the struggle against the colonization of African minds and bodies. A new generation of readers will rejoice upon learning, as my father did and wrote about, that they have been badly misled by academicians and organizers who proclaim to have created the blueprint on Black Power and who latched on to the Black Panther Party simply because they were out of ideas or acting on impulse. Those who previously settled for the seductive appetizer called "justice" will come to understand why Black Power as a concept and the Black Panther Party can never truly be interpreted by Hollywood.

Destroy This Temple will enlighten them to the root of the African fighting spirit.

Black Power!

Africa must be and will be free!

THIS BOOK

does not really need a dedication, but I hope that all those pioneer comrades, who have been with us for over ten years of struggle, and are still undaunted in their loyalty to the cause in the face of overwhelming odds, will read and enjoy it.

Destroy this temple, and in three days I will raise it up.

JOHN 2; 19

Contents

Introduction

THIS book is a love-letter, perhaps the most sincere love-letter I have ever written. The last time I referred to it in this manner, the man I was talking to nearly had a heart attack. What my friend found hard to understand was how an essay conceived and written in prison, and supported by other essays which did not profess love for my tormentors, could conceivably be said to have anything to do with love. I realised at once that I had a communication problem on my hands.

I had to explain to my friend what perhaps needs elaborating too for a lot of people, maybe not all of them White. To say you hate a murderer is only another way of saying you love the victim of his murder. At least, you love him enough to want him to live. In the same vein, a confession of disgust for the oppressor of a people is a declaration of love for the people who are at the receiving end of his oppression. A man who loves the suffering majority of mankind enough to hate the authors of their misery is a man motivated by love, not by hate. Therefore, to call such a man a hate-monger speaks more for the accuser than the accused. It is ironical therefore that it is always those people who so readily call Black Power activists advocates of hate who, when confronted with this choice between love and hate in one man, respond to hate by laying all the emphasis on it and react negatively to love which is the dominant component in the man. This book is motivated by love which I feel for all the oppressed peoples of this world; and to ask me to stop loving them is to ask me to start hating my mother and the majority of mothers in this world. It is a love-letter to my people, a record of my experiences so that those who will come after us will not have to run the gauntlet my generation has been through in order to learn the black-and-white facts of life.

But though these essays are based on the experiences of

my colleagues and myself, I want to make it absolutely clear that I do not consider myself a Black Power leader. Not only is the title pompous, undeserved and premature, it is a press invention. I may have played my part in pioneering activities or held positions of leadership in the Black Power movement; I prefer to regard these positions as purely administrative, not hierarchical. To echo the press and label oneself a Black leader is to *re*act rather than to act, and to meddle with the absolute right of the masses to choose their own leadership when they are ready. And before pundits start reading into this an indirect attack on other Black Power 'leaders', I want to state at once that any such suspicion is misguided; and I will go even further and assert my certainty that the other Black Power 'leaders' share my resentment and condemnation of this press interference in Black revolutionary concerns. What is important is not what a man is called but what he does and what difference his being alive makes to the people around him. In other words, ignore me, reader, I am not important. But don't ignore the realities reflected in this book. That is important, at least as important as the future of your children, and beyond.

On July 25th 1968 I was arrested and charged with masterminding a plot to murder White police officers in cold blood. Dragged out of bed in the dead hours of the morning by Scotland Yard custodians of law and order, I never saw my flat again till after six months of gruelling detention in Brixton Prison. I applied for bail five times and was refused bail five times. I was locked up in a cell twenty-three hours a day with little else for company but a plastic slop-bowl of my urine. There was no doubt in my mind I was going to be found guilty and, considering that the first of the three charges against me carried a maximum prison sentence of ten years alone, I was under no illusion I would be walking out of the Old Bailey a free man. My fear was justified on both counts. I was found guilty by an all-White jury, and given three years suspended sentence which is still hanging over my head. Of my two 'co-conspirators', who were being tried with me, one had absolute discharge, the other was fined fifty pounds suspended for three years, the levity of his sentence in comparison to mine being clear evidence of how I was portrayed, throughout the trial, as the corrupting arch-demon behind the Black Power 'conspiracy'. Charles Manson was a bit luckier in that, not wearing the devil's colour, he at least had the advantage of the onus being on the prosecution to prove that he was a demon, but in my own case, a Black man confronted with a London White jury whose daily vocabulary included such expressions as 'niggardly' and 'as black as sin', to mention but two, it went without saying that the onus was mine to prove that I was not a demon.

My arrest was based on a document which had come into the hands of the police. It was the pivot about which the entire case revolved. It is also to that document that I owe the inspiration for this volume. 'Destroy This Temple' is an essay which, though embracing the totality of Black experience in Britain, was written while in detention in prison primarily under the impetus of the document Unfortunately, we could not reprint this material here for reasons which can best be explained by lawyers. While I was able to persuade my publishers' lawyers that my possible immediate re-arrest should not concern them unduly, I was not successful in making them feel the same way about the equally probable prosecution of the publishers too for complicity in disseminating a writing which the arbiters of law and order have already branded a 'threat', not to mention the possible confiscation of the book, an eventuality which, apart from anything else, would in itself negate the very purpose of publication.

However, we must not make this loss sound more terrible than it is. All that the reader needs to know at this stage is that the original of this 'notorious' document was penned in my handwriting, and that the man who actually handed it over to the police was a black 'businessman' who happened to be the official printer of the Black Panther Movement in Britain at the time, and consequently was the printer of the magazine *Black Power Speaks*, which I edited.

I admit it could be described as a frightening document, depending of course on how you look at it. I admit it is not the sort of literature one reads to his little boy or girl at bedtime. Marked 'confidential' on top of this, it was doomed from the start in a society where the getting together of two or three Black people behind closed doors is considered invasion of White privacy and rape of the peace of mind of the 'silent majority'. As the prosecution aptly summarised it in court, this piece of writing was not designed to humour Detective Chief Inspector Thompson and his colleagues in the Yard.

Every time it was read out in court, gasps of horror invariably erupted from certain sections of the public gallery, and even the most unflappable of lawyers would crane their necks round to regard me as if I were some piece of human refuse in the dock. Every time the prosecuting counsel read out the 'ghastliest' selected passages from it to oppose yet another of my applications for bail before the Judge in Chambers—and they always made a point of reading them— you could almost feel the judge fighting hard to restrain himself from slapping my face before ordering me back to prison.

For this reason, many of my friends and supporters were anxious to point out that I did not in fact write the offending document. But when it became evident that the police were in possession of the original document in my handwriting, everybody was desperately asserting that I did not share the sentiments expressed in it and that, though I was the author of the piece, it was not intended for publication in that form. Two leading QC's, Mr Kellock and Sir Dingle Foot, plus a leading advocate, Mr Hassan, were lined up to defend me and my two partners in 'crime'. There were countless demonstrations on our behalf, culminating in one right outside Brixton Prison itself, on Jebb Avenue, organised by a group from Birmingham led by Margaret Gardener, the police dutifully doing their thing too with truncheons. These demonstrations were made in various forms and on different levels. Writing in his weekly column 'Shouts and Murmurs' in the *Observer* on November 17th, this is what Kenneth Tynan had to say:

Obi Egbuna, the gifted young Nigerian novelist (*Wind*

Versus Polygamy, Faber and Faber), playwright (*The Anthill*, broadcast on BBC TV) and Black Power leader, has now been in Brixton Prison for four months without trial. During that period he has been refused bail four times: a few weeks ago he learned that the Biafran village where he was born (and where many members of his family still live) had been destroyed in the civil war. Together with two other men, he was arrested in July and charged with 'uttering a writing threatening to kill police officers at Hyde Park'. As the interval lengthens between arrest and trial, his friends are naturally anxious to know what this 'writing' could possibly be; and if the evidence against Egbuna has any substance, it is about time he was confronted with it in open court. I am delighted to hear that Andrew Faulds, the Labour MP, has tabled a question on the case for the Home Secretary to answer. Before his arrest Egbuna was working on a new play about Enoch Powell . . . a mock trial, I'm told . . . the manuscript of which was seized by the cops. Without presuming to comment on the rights and wrongs of a case that is still sub judice, I can't help recalling the Roman mob in *Julius Caesar*, who couldn't distinguish between Cinna the poet and Cinna the politician. Let us hope that the police know the difference between Egbuna the dramatist and Egbuna the black militant. Politically he is a socialist who believes that revolution in Africa cannot be achieved without violence. This dismays him, because he finds violence repulsive. But he asks us, in one of his pamphlets, to look at the word from a black point of view:

'It is very difficult for many liberal intellectuals to understand that violence is not always accompanied by the boom of guns and the clatter of bayonets. When a little African boy is compelled to die of starvation in a world where there is abundance, I call it violence. When an old black man in Harlem is made by his fellow men to live all his days sharing dingy tenements with rats, I call that violence. When I see that Africa is the richest continent in the world and Africans are the poorest people on the same planet, I call that violence . . . And when I see that the leather of my English landlord's shoes could be from my home, the material of his clothes mine, the stick of his rolled umbrella mine, the copper of his cigarette case and the tobacco in it too mine, when I see that even the manganese of his industry and the oil that runs the machines are all from my home, while my own mother . . . a woman who, judging by the standards of her faraway English dependants, should be living like a queen . . . is in fact living on the hunger line, I call that violence.'

Kenneth Tynan has quoted me correctly. Apart from one or two minor inaccuracies in factual details, his general observations on this case are quite cogent. He is right when he says I am not a violent man. But what I find hard to take is the subtle suggestion, and in making it he is not alone, that a good Black man is the one who finds resort to arms to get rid of oppression 'repulsive'. He implies that no intelligent Black man could have written such a 'violent' document, and that even if I had done it, it had to be a case of the good Egbuna, which is of course Egbuna the dramatist, the complete negation of Egbuna the Black militant, producing it as a 'mock' activity. No doubt he meant well. No doubt they all meant well who tried to use this line of argument to help me. But what I find downright insulting, and definitely 'repulsive', is their typically liberal logic that violence is excusable in a Black man only when he uses it in crawling under a limbo bar. The underlying presumption is that it is all right if the Black man's struggle against racial aggression is limited to mock trials, mock resistance, mock declaration of war. But the moment this struggle is elevated to the realm of revolutionary reality, it becomes a crime. Violence—being of course the ultimate question of the Black and White confrontation—is a subject I have given adequate coverage in later pages of this book.

My main concern in this introduction is to put the reader in the picture regarding why and where and what this book is about.

Since I came out of jail, I have, for reasons which will

become clearer as we proceed, recoiled into a position of relative political silence which of course has not been too easy. It has not been easy because a team of mysterious campaigners, not all of them blond and blue-eyed, have launched a systematic carefully-planned attack aimed not just at misrepresenting the aim and philosophy of the Black Power movement, but mainly, it would seem, at discrediting and denigrating its interpreters and activists, employing the whole art of imagery to alienate them from the Black masses. Though this campaign has only succeeded in producing the very opposite effect in the Black communities, the undisguised vindictiveness and professional inventiveness behind the personal attacks on, for some reason, me in particular, have so enraged those associates who have been very close to us in the struggle over the years, that some of them have taken for granted that the first time I broke my long political silence, it would be in a slashing counter-attack exposing these self-appointed saints and demonologists of Black militants. I am afraid I am going to disappoint all those who share the expectations of these well-meaning associates. While I feel flattered by their confidence, and moved by their loyalty to the cause, we must not allow ourselves to be goaded into losing sight of the priorities.

As far as counter-attacking and exposing those misinformed and misguided Black men who are taking part in this anti-Black campaign is concerned, we must remind ourselves that the first discipline of a mature political activist is to make sure, no matter how tempting the contrary may sometimes be, that the blow he is aiming at the enemy does not fall on the head of one of his own brothers. I think this is what distinguishes the men from the boys. And as far as counter-attacking the White ones is concerned, we must also remind ourselves that we owe them neither apologies nor explanations. The number one rule about an apology is that the person to whom one is apologising is in a moral position to be a recipient of that apology; and, even with the most generous of allowances, I cannot be persuaded that a man motivated solely by expediency can impeach any man of my historical background on matters of morality, not even one of my sinful standards.

No, my dialogue here is not with my accusers. The last time I spoke to them was at the Old Bailey, and that was under duress. That relationship ceased to exist the moment I stepped out of the court room. My dialogue in these pages is with my fellow 'grinning piccaninnies', wherever they may be.

We never claim to be angels. On the contrary, we have maintained over the years that any political activist who claims to be an angel may not find it an easy job explaining to himself, let alone his comrades, why he deems it necessary to make a revolution to change the society which produces angels like himself. The greatest let-down of the Black revolution, whether in Africa or elsewhere, has always come from the self-appointed angel class. That is why we say to-day that the golden age of the angel class is over. The Black revolution will become a reality only when it is made by the shit class.

The history of Black Power in Britain is the history of the shit class trying to organise themselves. It was not until Stokely Carmichael's historic visit in the summer of 1967, when he came to participate in the Dialectics of Liberation seminar at the Round House, that Black Power got a foothold in Britain. In fact, even on the very afternoon he made his first address at Speakers Corner, as he was ascending the platform, some of the present leaders of the Black Power groups were attacking Black Power as an extremist concept. I was there. This is more of a reflection on the society that had for years put blinkers on the eyes of its Black community, isolating them from the rest of the Black world, than on the boys themselves who, by the way, must be congratulated for their quick rate of ideological growth and courage in admitting their error when they discovered they were wrong.

It was one of the best speeches I have ever heard Stokely make, and his impact on the audience, both Black and White, was electric. By the time he finished speaking, it had become evident that, if he was lucky enough to get away from Britain without being arrested, he was destined to be banned from coming back. A new phase of Black history had begun.

Eighteen months before that, I had returned from the American visit which I have described in one of the main essays later, in my letter to Dolores, the Black prostitute of Harlem. Though I had become involved in Black Power ideology by then, and was always explaining the significance of my badge (brought back from the States) whenever I wore it to Black meetings, there was no Black Power organisation in Britain. The nearest to it was Michael Malik's Racial Adjustment Action Society (RAAS), but even that, as far as I knew, was a (Black) Muslim group, nearer to Elijah Muhammad's American Black Nation of Islam than Black Power as I had come to understand it. It has of course progressed since then.

Very few Black people knew what Black Power was, and the converts to it were even fewer. The press did not help, because, for obvious reasons, they had insistently defined it as the Black counterpart of the Ku-Klux-Klan, something as exclusively American as the apple pie. Our few attempts to even find an audience for its discussion in Britain met with unspeakable opposition. Never underrate the enemy. His groundwork had been thorough. That was our first lesson.

The dominant 'immigrant' organisation in Britain then was Campaign Against Racial Discrimination (CARD), modelled after the late Martin Luther King's Southern Christian Leadership Conference (SCLC) in the States. Knowing the history of the Black Power movement in America, that it began by splitting from the SCLC, we were not too surprised that members of CARD reacted coldly towards the 'irresponsible' and non-pacifist advocates of Black Power. This was the case with most Black organisations. To be fair, there were a number of militant and dedicated small Black organisations within which devoted Garveyists were working round the clock; but, at a time when it was considered the climax of absurdity to call a 'West Indian' African, they attracted very little membership, and none of them naturally emerged into an organisation of national stature. The only organisations that made it were liberal and 'integrationist'. The easiest way to get thrown out of any of the 'respectable' Black meetings was to walk in with a

B

Black Power badge pinned on your jacket. I don't think we can ever forget our experience when a few of us attended the Lambeth Party's annual-dinner ball at Brixton Town Hall and were recognised by our badge. This does not mean that there were no Leftist-orientated Blacks who would have made potential Black Power recruits. On the contrary, there were many of them but, mostly students, the majority were so steeped in infantile Lefticism, thanks to the Socialist Party of Great Britain, that they found it tough to appreciate the ideological and dialectical up-to-dateness of the Black Power philosophy.

So, biding our time, we contented ourselves with our old activities in the Pan-African movement. And anyway, as the editor of *United Africa,* the then voice of the Council of African Organisations, based at the African Unity House, No. 3 Collingham Gardens, I had more than plenty to occupy my time.

Stokely's arrival was like manna from heaven. But I was not prepared for the speed at which things were to happen. I had been invited on-stage to join the panel of speakers and to introduce Stokely Carmichael to the audience on the night he addressed the Black community at the Round House. My theme was that the time had come when the Black people must stop moaning about what was wrong and organise to start doing what was right. I made one or two suggestions. A few days later, I was invited to the annual general meeting of the Universal Coloured Peoples Association (UCPA) in a church-hall in Ladbroke Grove. Before I knew what was happening, the organisation had voted unanimously to adopt the Black Power ideology and I was elected as the chairman. Black Power had come to Britain.

Perhaps it was a sign of things to come that the White girl who was the acting secretary of the out-going committee was so infuriated at the way things had turned out that she walked up to me right after the meeting and handed me a broom to start sweeping the floor, as her house-boy, to leave the militants in no doubt what she thought of us and our Black Power 'insanity'. She liked it even less when I accepted the broom with smile and gratitude and used it to demonstrate how unity is strength and how it could be employed to sweep away the foot-prints of an arrogant adversary, especially when the components of this unity were as weak and tiny as broomsticks.

The first thing we did was to rescue the UCPA from Speakers Corner and take it into the ghetto. Then we launched our manifesto, *Black Power in Britain*, which still speaks for itself, and not just for its historical significance to-day.

Then our troubles began. Our first shock was to discover that we were too much of a mixed bag to constitute one political movement. Within that single organisation, there were members who believed that the answer to the Black man's problem lay in the overthrow of the capitalist system, and there were others who felt it lay in the Black man going to the House of Lords; there were some who saw themselves as part of international Black revolution, and there was a faction who believed that the Black man in this country should concern himself only with what goes on in this country; consequently, while some preferred to see the Black population of Britain returning home ultimately to spearhead revolutions in the home countries, others maintained that our main role here should be helping to secure jobs, houses, acceptance and integration into the British system for our two million Blacks till they eventually become English in every way but colour; while some saw the education the Black students are getting in this country as a weapon of anti-Black neo-colonialism, others saw it as the Black man's only road to power; while some believed in fraternising with White political activists, others were dead against it; while some favoured demonstrations as means of political action, others saw them as a childish waste of time; while some wanted us to become an underground movement and fight for what we want 'by every means necessary', others thought this was too 'extreme' and preferred to see us as a Left-wing non-violent organisation; while some believed in going all out to mobilise the Black masses in Britain as a matter of urgency, others opposed it as strategic suicide, maintaining that priority must first be given to building up an impregnable and dependable core before we could make any move to the masses; in short, it became all too clear that what we had was not one movement, but movements within a movement. We did not all belong to one organisation.

The worst part was that these differences in ideological orientation were not limited to the ordinary members of the group; they were even more pronounced in the 'core'. Soon it became impossible to reach decisions at meetings. Every faction saw every issue on the agenda from its own ideological view-point, and the views were as irreconcilable as heaven and hell. Sometimes, we would spend weeks debating a most insignificant item of policy, only to drop it in the end because we could not reach a decision.

It was not as if we were not working hard. We worked literally round the clock, met constantly and, during our campaign of 'going to the people', we used to meet every night at seven o'clock and start tramping the streets of Brixton, Ladbroke Grove or whichever ghetto was scheduled for our field-work of the season, and start knocking from door to door, distributing leaflets, selling our manifesto, and talking to people. The response was tremendous, but the divisions between us prevented us from taking advantage of the situation. The new recruits who attended our meetings for the first time were so horrified by the snarling and bickering that went on that they never showed up again. Meetings became more and more impossible as things grew from bad to worse. It became so laughable it wasn't funny.

Meanwhile, members of the out-voted old committee, still embittered at the 'extremist take-over', reorganised and turned up at our public meetings to disrupt them. The police had not been idle either. Taking advantage of our disunity, they began to arrest us one by one, and hardly a night would pass without a Black Power man sleeping in a cell. When we were not being bailed, we were at the police station anyway arranging bail for others. I was up at all hours of the night. My landlady wondered if it would not be a better idea to ask the postman to deliver all my registered mail at the police station. She was not being funny. This was not the only way we were being taunted by agents of law and order. Black informers and trained disruptionists began to appear at our meetings. I can now see them in retrospect. They were the 'ultra-militant' ones who shouted loudest and started all the fights. Their main aim was to disrupt the movement under the guise of uncompromising militancy, and to eliminate genuine militants marked by the Establishment as the real threats to them, by accusing and 'exposing' them as traitors, informers and crooks who collected money from embassies behind our backs. Oh, they were beautiful. They did a superb job and deserved every penny they were paid.

They were so successful that, before long, our purely ideological conflicts had degenerated into bitter conflicts of personalities; and the precious time, which we ought to have spent organising Black people to fight a common oppressor, was wasted away in producing leaflets of accusations and counter-accusations. Mistaking our lack of willingness to participate in this infantile notion of revolution as weakness, two other UCPAs emerged at the same time, each claiming to be the genuine movement and to have launched the official manifesto, the original of which was of course in my handwriting. This was too much. Fleet Street declared this as the proof of the Black's man's inherent inability to unite with his fellow Black man.

As things reached these lamentable proportions, there was only one thing to do. Our annual general meeting was not due till October. We called it prematurely in April. I resigned both chairmanship and membership of the UCPA and, when nominated again, refused re-election. Webb, the secretary, did the same. Before leaving the meeting, I had announced the formation of a Black Panther Movement in Britain.

We began the Panthers with only three or four members, but we had learnt from the old UCPA that what really mattered was not the number of beginners, but the ideological unity, mutual trust and solidarity of purpose which would cement the core together and the discipline and maturity with which they were prepared to implement it. It is still my belief that the secret of the Panthers' success to date, even if limited, lies in this insistence, from the very dawn of its formation, that the movement must be a fraternity of brothers of strictly identical ideological orientation.

Though we were so few we could have held our meetings in a telephone box if we had wished, the degree of solidarity between us was so great we felt that, had we actually done so, we should not have attracted attention because it would have been like one man standing there. It worked like magic. Our ideological oneness and unflinching dedication to the cause became so infectious that Pantherism soon began to spread like wild-fire.

To consolidate our solidarity, we introduced a few measures which I need not go into here. Suffice it to say that no new recruit could be a full member till after six months of probation during which he would have to fulfil certain set tasks and prove his sincerity in more ways than by regular attendance of meetings. The immediately recognisable difference between us and the old UCPA was that, while in the old association we were always begging people to join us and ever grateful when they complied, people queued up to join the new Panther group and were proud to be accepted as peripheral probational members.

This was the time when we launched the 'notorious' monthly magazine *Black Power Speaks*, to spell out where the Panthers stood. During my Old Bailey trial, the jury was bored again and again with passages from articles in successive issues of this magazine, the prosecution plugging and plugging relentlessly the point that no 'respectable' Black man, only a wicked one, would ever be at the centre of such double 'crime'. To be the founder-chairman of the 'evil' movement could be considered excusable carelessness, but to be the founder-editor of the 'evil' magazine as well was the last straw of inexcusable criminality.

It was not just I who was on trial. It was the Panther movement. It was the magazine. The Establishment's fear was not shammed. It was real. They were horrified at what impact the months-old magazine was making in Black communities. It was hardly a glamorous magazine, but it was choking with truth. It told Black people the truth about themselves. It had to die. After the third issue, rumours reached us that a decision had been taken to kill it.

Not long after that, a few days after I had come back from Conakry with Osagyefo Nkrumah's personal message to the Black peoples of Britain, I was arrested.

When I was released from jail six months later, I began to notice that things were not quite the same in the Panthers. What I found on my return was no longer the organisation for which I had seen the heart of Babylon, and for which I would have gladly given my life. New influences were definitely at work; I could sense it. One or two 'ultra-militants', none of whom by our old standards would have qualified even for probational membership of the Panthers, had, out of the blue, made their way to the very centre of the core, and had goaded the boys into reversing the very ideological beliefs which had been the cornerstone of the Panther magic. Everything was upside down. Our attitude to a number of things had changed: namely our stand on White radicals, demonstrations, oath-taking, the sanctity of the core, even the very concept of probational membership had been ruled out, and anybody could stroll in at will. Quarrelling and snarling which I had never known in the Panther brotherhood became a common occurrence at the very core of the movement, worse than the UCPA of old. Distrust, backbiting, and secret factional meetings in which personalities were discussed became the order of the day. I looked on the faces of brothers where before I had seen nothing but love and the glow of revolutionary sublimity, and they had now become barren slates on which evil hands had scribbled unrevolutionary obscenities, hate, suspicion, and the greatest enemy of a fighter: fear. Tears stood in my eyes and, for once, I opened my mouth and words dried in my throat.

Rumours which had reached me in prison, and which I had discounted as false, began to echo in my ears with an ominous ring of truth. Under the most childish of guises, someone had been holding meetings in my absence to delude the boys into stabbing us in the back. Less than two weeks after I came out of jail, I had been summoned twice before the new core to account for my 'lax' political activities and inconstancy in attendance of meetings which I did not even know had taken place. I could not think of what crime I had committed except having suffered for the cause. I asked the old boys what was happening and those who found voice to answer me back opened their mouths and what came out was not their voice, but someone else's. Even then, it was a voice tremulous with guilt and shame. I knew that they had been taken unawares by forces beyond their control, and by the time they knew which way the wind was blowing, it was too late. They had crossed the Rubicon. I also suspected that the only reason my chairmanship had not been challenged was fear that I might split, as I did from the old UCPA, and start another organisation. And since I had just come out of jail and was something of a martyred hero in the eyes of the Black communities, it was a gamble no one dared take, at least not while the news of my incarceration was still fresh in the minds of our people. If any one had any doubts, the Black turn-out at the Mock Trial of Enoch Powell in Brixton, the only public political activity I had organised since my release, dispelled them. The response of the Black community was tremendous; workers, students, writers, lawyers, actors, representatives of different political organisations, all sorts of people who would not have come together, under different circumstances, gathered under one roof to mock Enoch Powell. The atmosphere was electric. While the National Front was demonstrating outside, the voice of Andrew Salkey intoning poetry on the stage, the gravel voice of Ram John Holder was grinding out soul in the background. I have never heard Black youths from the ghettoes make more revolutionary speeches and appeals for unity as I heard that day.

Yet in the thick of this triumph for our people, my heart was heavy with pain, for I knew that a heavy cloud was hanging over the Panther movement and the history of the old UCPA was about to repeat itself. At least, in the old UCPA, I knew what was going wrong as it was happening. But in the present dilemma of the Panthers, while I knew that some evil forces were at work, I had no idea what they were; and even when I could guess what these hidden forces were, I could not tell exactly where the strings were being pulled and how many enemies had infiltrated the organisation. The enemy was not always the British Intelligence. The South Africans, not to mention the proverbial American CIA, have been known to spare no expenses in their London witch-hunting of potential enemies of tomorrow, and have a reputation for being more ruthless in disrupting organisations than the more sophisticated and subtle British. To add insult to injury, a certain character, a so-called member of the new core, a man who was not even a Panther before I went to prison, had broken into my home while I was away, unknown to others, and committed a crime for which no man could ever forgive another. But seeing that I was not put away for years as he had hoped, and terrified that I might expose him by bringing the whole thing into the open, he tried to forestall me by circulating false rumours, accusing me, before I could accuse him, of the very unforgivable crime he himself had committed against me while I was behind bars. Unfortunately for the poor rat, I have been around too long, and he soon learned that he was preaching to an audience who had been reading me like a book for the past ten years and knew, though I was a 'criminal', what sort of crime I was capable of committing. Even among those who even to-day do not know the full facts behind the anti-Obi campaign, there are very few, and I have yet to meet them, who gave credence to these wild fabrications.

Nevertheless, I found enough wrong in the Panthers to persuade me to rethink my position. There were three courses of action open to me: to plunge headlong and start fighting hidden forces which I did not quite understand, or to resign from the Panthers altogether and, starting from scratch, form another new organisation along the lines of the Panthers, an organisation such as we originally envisaged, or lastly to recoil into temporary political oblivion and, in distant hibernation, survey the grounds, study the forces at work, and regenerate myself. Of these three possible courses of action, the first struck me as being singularly naïve, for only a genius or a fool would venture to take up arms against an adversary whom he does not quite understand; the second, for very personal reasons, appealed to me even less—even if I had wanted to, there simply wasn't time to start organising a new political movement at this stage of my stay in England, and, besides, I don't really care much for splits if there is an alternative; which finally left me with the last choice, which was to go into voluntary exile for a while and maintain political silence—which brings us back where we came in.

I hope I have not given the impression that, in the Black Power movement, we are perpetually in a state of siege, or that I have given up the struggle. On the contrary, this is only the beginning of the struggle. As I have explained elsewhere, at this stage of our development, internal conflicts of this nature are inevitable, sometimes necessary. The surprise is that we have as few as we do at the moment.

I have not pointed these conflicts out because I want to discredit or denigrate anyone. What I hope I have highlighted is what low level of animalistic and suicidal practices of self-hatred an oppressive society can make an oppressed people inflict on each other, brother stabbing brother in the back, father informing on son, men selling their soul for a pint of stale ale, like the slave who would kill other slaves as an alternative to losing his own life, or the Jew employed to murder fellow Jews in concentration camps as a price for life and liberty. I am not rebuking the victim; I am merely describing the symptoms of his infection. Only that way can it be cured, or avoided in future. If someone somewhere, especially among those who will come after us, learns something useful from our experience, then every pain I have suffered and every second I have spent behind bars has been worth it.

I would not have written half the things I have written here if I had not already come to terms again with most of the comrades and brothers I have talked about in these pages. Some of them, particularly the secretary of the original core of our pioneer Panther group who, perhaps more than anybody else, shocked me with his change of attitude when I first came out of jail, have become even closer comrades to me now than they ever were before and, in fact, number among those close revolutionary friends whom I had in mind when I was writing my dedication. We live in a world of live and learn, and when a man is big enough to say he is sorry, you should be humble enough to say all is forgiven, especially when you know that you too might have reacted the way he did to offend you if the same pressure and heat had been turned on you under the same circumstances.

Both the Panthers and the UCPA are to-day resplendent with young bloods who were not around when these things happened. And even among those who were around, very few of them actually knew what was going on behind the scenes.

These young bloods, probably because most of them have come from the shit class which we have already mentioned, are showing signs of doing great things and no doubt will go a long way. Perhaps unconsciously, or maybe in accordance with the natural law of retribution, if you are that superstitious, these boys long ago began to get rid of those invidious and divisive elements which were responsible for our early set-backs in the Panthers, to pick up the spirit of the revolutionary responsibility which the Panther pioneers had in mind. It is always a pleasure to welcome them to my home for our little 'chats'; and it will be an even greater pleasure to welcome them home in Africa in the near future under circumstances in which I could genuinely call Africa my home.

Meanwhile, there is a lot to be done. They too have some organising to do. This is no place to start telling them what Black Power is. It has been defined in the appropriate place. But we would do well to remember that Black Power is not emotion. We must reject emotion because emotion cannot be trusted. It cannot be trusted because it does not last. Emotion can induce you to break into a police station to try to free a Black brother from a cell. But short-sighted as it is, what emotion does not make you see is that, unless it is a well-organised operation, planned with maps to the minutest detail, not only will you fail to secure the release of the arrested brother from the police cell, you will be putting nine more brothers in the same cell as well, the difference being that you have only succeeded in multiplying your original problem ten times over; that is, 1,000 per cent profit in self-injury, the only kind of profit-making which the enemies of the Black revolution will encourage the Black man to specialise in with their eternal blessing. The only answer is organisation, based on a cool and passionless analysis of the problem in hand. Such organisation in the hands of ten serious-minded people is a more powerful weapon than ten thousand cannons in the hands of ten thousand emotional buffoons. That is why lack of organisation has been the bane of the two million-strong Blacks of Britain. I know. I ought to know.

For a whole fortnight in December 1968, I crawled out of my cell every morning, chained (or hand-cuffed as it is called nowadays) and taken to the Old Bailey like a beast, in a vehicle on which a cow-van would be an improvement, and was expected to prove that I am not a racist, before twelve White men whose only qualification to the jury-box was each having capitalised enough from institutionalised racism* (which has castrated my people for centuries) to own a property. I resented having to do this. And what I resented even more was the fact that, as long as the Black man in this country was unorganised, I had no choice. To play the Black Bat Man without even a Robin at my age struck me as the poorest imitation of White self-overestimation. To play the heroic martyr in a situation which was in desperate need of live activists rather than martyrs was no act of heroism, but recklessness. I take great pains to point this out, not in order to brag about the wisdom of my stand or even to cover the lack of it, but for the simple reason that it is about time Black people started remembering a fact which their detractors would rather have them forget, namely, that one of the tragedies of the Black struggle, especially of recent years, is that it has produced more martyrs than activist leaders who

---

*In the movement we recognise two types of racism—Individual Racism and Institutionalised Racism. The former, which I have *not* accused the jury of, consists in individual acts of racism, e.g. discrimination. The latter consists in being, consciously or unconsciously, a beneficiary of political institutions that practise racial oppression through exploitation, colonialism, neo-colonialism, etc.

lived to achieve their goal.

This is a fast-moving world; so fast that by the time you shut your eyes and open them again, promising a lady a slice of the moon as a sign of gallantry may sound as ridiculous as offering her the bark of a tree because every lab is choking with moon-samples; and where offering a girlfriend a wedding ring to cement your love may earn you a slap in the face for threatening with menace because marriage has become laughably out-of-date. Naturally, it is not only in Black Power circles that things have been happening since I came out of jail and since these essays were written. Fortunately, the way things are turning out, far from invalidating my analysis, have proved me uncannily right and, in fact, made the essays even more relevant now than when they were written.

We have seen Powellism, which began as a British government strategy to invalidate the Commonwealth status as a prelude to joining the European Common Market, developing into a national movement in which the British people, as if pulled by an invisible force, are unconsciously digging the grave for millions of British children yet unborn. If it were in Germany that a man like Powell were to get up and start talking about the birth-rate of the non-White population being a danger to White people, the Germans, from their history, would be intelligent enough at least to understand what he was saying. They would know that the next logical step would be a definition of who is the White man. And in a country like Britain, where the majority of the population have the Black man's eyes, the Black man's nose, the Black man's hair, and even the Black man's bone-structure (i.e., contrary to the fascist definition of 'the White man', the majority of the British population are not blond and blue-eyed), I should have thought that the British 'White man' would be the last White man to want that definition to be drawn. Bearing in mind what happened the last time such a definition took place in Europe, and not wilfully blinding ourselves to the fact that any time a British 'White man' goes to the continent, especially to a Scandinavian country where the majority of the population are blond and blue-eyed, and starts throwing his weight about as a 'White man', he usually provokes a giggle when he turns his back, I should have thought that if the British 'White man' succeeds in persuading Europe to take Powellism seriously and follow it up with the inevitable question who is the White man within the next generation or two, this will be an invitation to a repetition of Hitlerism and history in which the heads of yet-unborn British generations will roll.

But perhaps it is in the case of Nigeria that the march of events is proving me more right than even I had feared. In the essay 'A Word About My Home', I have analysed the situation in Nigeria; and, though the Biafran war was still on when I was writing, the way the war has ended and the progress of events in the country to-day have conclusively proved this essay more pertinent to-day perhaps than when it was written. For example, it made little sense when I described the war as an imperialist war while the 'Nigerian' and 'Biafran' soldiers were still shooting at each other. But, as every Nigerian knows to-day, if he were to dig up the bodies of all the soldiers killed in that war, he can no longer tell which body was 'Nigerian' and which was 'Biafran', because all the tribal marks, whether Ibo, Yoruba, or Hausa, have perished with the flesh of the soldiers that bore them. The Ibos, the Yorubas and the Hausas have become indistinguishable in the grave. Just one people! But there is one thing which remains distinguishable and indestructible, and will remain there long after the bodies have perished and rotted away. And that is the bullet that killed the soldiers. Every one of these corpses carries that same bullet, made in one White country or another. What becomes evident is that the bullet which killed both the Ibo and the Hausa came from the same source, the same man. That man is enemy to both of them. That is how the Nigerian masses have come to identify the true enemy of the people. No man allows his bullet to be shot into you if he considers you his friend. The bullet is the mark of the conqueror, and that signature speaks for itself to-day in the graves of the sons of Nigeria killed in the war. This is a category which overrides tribe, sex, or religion. It is the reality and the woe of Nigeria.

If I sound a little divisionist here in terms of Black and White, I hope the reason will not be too hard to grasp. There are three things pain does for a man. The first springs from the psychology of man itself which shows that man never really thinks unless he has a problem. The second is that pain gives man the courage to stop identifying himself with those who cause him suffering. Finally, I have come to the conclusion that without pain, life itself would be unendurable. I have tried to imagine what life would be like without problems and how I would feel if I had the best house in the world, the best wardrobe in the world, the best farm in the world, the most beautiful wife in the world, the homeliest family in the world, the loveliest children in the world, the richest library in the world, the very best of everything worthwhile in the world; I tried divining in the dinginess of my prison cell what life would mean to me if I had all these things, and I came to the conclusion that such a life must be hell. The thought that one day I would die and leave all these beautiful things behind would be enough to drive anyone insane. Yet, death is the only certainty there is in life. Death is the ultimate fate of all men, the 'undiscovered country from whose bourn no traveller returns'. Any man who cannot come to terms with this reality cannot face life. And that is precisely what would befall man without pain. Pain gives man wisdom to know himself, guts to fight his aggressor, and maturity to cope with the awful idea of dying. We fight the oppressors of our people, not because we are cowards towards pain, but to live to organise it so that our people need not have more than their own share of it, as they have done for far far too long. Pain is like food: in sufficient quantities, it is essential for survival; in excessive dosage, it incapacitates and destroys.

I know that other peoples too have had more than their own dose of suffering. I deplore it as much I deplore the suffering of my people. But what I deplore even more is that those other people would rather add to my misery than get rid of their own. I think it is a shame that the self-appointed architects of world civilisation have created a world where a man born in Leamington Spa is no longer

just a human being with wife and kids to look after, but a
'White bastard'; and where another man born in Bulawayo
with his own wife and kids to cater for is equally not just
another human being, but a 'Black bastard'. But what I
think an even bigger shame is that, in the company of the
'bastard' of Bulawayo, the 'bastard' of Leamington Spa,
rather than see the absurdity of man's devaluation by man,
would prefer to create an aristocracy of bastards to further
devalue man.

I now come to the end of this introduction. This is not
the first literature on Black Power in Britain. It may be the
first book. It will not be the last. I do not pretend to have
supplied all the answers. On the contrary, I am sure that if
someone else were asked to give his own account of these
events, particularly the odd 'militant' whose methods and
motives I have called in question, their versions of the same
story would probably come out different. I do not grudge
them their views, or their right to be entitled to them.
However, since what is in question here is not my political
love affairs, but how 'Egbuna the dramatist', after originally
travelling across half the world to secure 'education' in good
old 'civilised' England, suddenly found himself at the Old
Bailey being tried for plotting to overthrow the very system
that has given him that 'education', what is relevant here is
what went 'wrong', how that chasm was bridged, my own
experience, and how I evaluate it. In other words, I have
tried in this book to verbalise what is not really verbal, to
communicate, through a series of essays, the thunder and
lightning in my soul. I offer no apologies for the quality of
my voice. Like Frantz Fanon, 'I want my voice to be harsh,
I don't want it to be beautiful, I don't want it to be pure, I
don't want it to have all dimensions. I want it to be torn
through and through, I don't want it to be enticing, for I
am speaking of man and his refusal, of the day-to-day rotten-
ness of man, of his dreadful failure. I want you to tell.'

A few days after I came out of jail, Ted Joans, the great
Afro-American painter and jazz poet, 'a nomad in the arts
as well as in the physical world', on the way to one of his
many treks to Africa, gave a moving poetry recital at the

Africa Centre in London. But the poem that brought tears to my eyes that night was not the one he dedicated to our many years of friendship; it was another beautiful piece which he called simply 'The Truth'. I would like to reproduce it here as a bridge between this introduction and the main body of the book; because, for me, it summarises the agony, the loneliness, and the unrequited solicitations of many a Black Power activist as recently as five years ago in this country:

> If you should see a man
> walking down a crowded street
> talking aloud to himself,
> don't run in the opposite direction;
> but run toward him
> for he is a poet.
> You have nothing to fear from a poet,
> but the TRUTH.

Note to the Jury

I MUST start with a warning. Some things I am going to state in this book will strike some people as 'extreme'. It has been my experience that every time a Black man tries to conduct a frank, intelligent and unvarnished discussion about race, he is automatically branded as a pessimist 'extremist'. It often turns out though that, far from being a pessimist, he is only a realist in the company of optimists. Meanwhile, the presumption of course is that putting a label on a man whose case you find unanswerable automatically invalidates his case.

It does not worry me being labelled 'extremist'. I have been in prison long enough not to care any more what names people call me. Goodness knows, I have been called frightful names in my time. Why, only last night in this prison, a man actually called me a christian. I forgave him.

My only reason for starting with this warning is to bring into focus at the outset a fact which often conveniently eludes our accusers. It also eludes the liberal demonologists who label every Black man who refuses to let them do his thinking for him 'extremist'. Such a Black man is encroaching upon their preserve—the interpretation and moulding of the Black mind. The truth is that 'extremism' is strictly a relative term. It is a word you can employ only in a situation which offers alternatives. It is a term which presupposes choice; it implies that a man to whom it is applied has more than one possibility from which to choose. So the existence of possible alternatives to a course of action must be an essential constituent of a situation before you can properly qualify that course of action as 'extreme'. Something cannot be 'extreme' unless it is extreme relative to something else.

Therefore, when a man has a problem and it is proved that he has tried out, and exhausted without success, all alternative means of tackling that problem except one, anyone who calls that remaining course of action 'extreme' is either naïve or, much more likely, does not, consciously or unconsciously, wish that man to solve his problem. This is how we must judge that Black man today, or not judge him at all. Before we can call a Black militant 'extremist' today, we must first and foremost investigate and ascertain that he does indeed have alternative courses of action to the one he takes. Before we can find a Black man guilty of violence and 'unnecessary extremism', which in effect is what my accusers are asking you, the jury, to do, we must first find out whether or not I do have any justification to be frustrated with such advertised alternatives as Gandhi's 'Passive Resistance' and Luther King's 'Coalition of Conscience'. Which is why I must now begin with an essay that examines this question, and the practical application of Gandhism to the growing confrontation between the Black man and the White man. Then I must follow this essay up with three others which deal respectively with the Black man and himself, the Black man and the White woman, and the Black man and the Black woman, in that order. And having thus acquainted you, jury, with these different dimensions of the Black personality of today, we shall then return to a consideration of our 'murder plot' leaving you with a better knowledge of the prisoner in the dock.

Black Power or Death

(Written when I was UCPA Chairman)

FOR MOST people, the death of Martin Luther King must be the end of an illusion. Like Martin, they dreamt dreams, which have suddenly become a nightmare. Like him, they went to the mountain top and saw whiteness without recognising it as the whiteness of snow capping a volcano of blood. Today that volcano has erupted and, with it, the ugly truth that the answer to White racism is not dreams and the singing of hymns.

Expectedly, many beautiful and glowing obituaries have been written about Martin, and countless books have been churned out to extol his greatness and magnanimity of purpose. And no Black man in his right senses can deny that Martin, our Black brother mowed down by a White fascist assassin's bullet, deserves our tears. But while we cry we must not allow ourselves to be dazed by our own tears and, under the subtle persuasion of White liberal sentimentalists, let our timely venom and keyed-up revolutionary energies be sublimated into obituary sing-songs epitomising the sanctity of dreams.

What we, the living, must now concern ourselves with is to find out at once what lessons to learn from Martin's life and the manner of his death. We must let the liberals and sentimentalists carry on with sweet obituaries and the reading of Psalms, for we have a job to do. And that job is to lay our dead brother on a mortuary slab and subject him to a passionless and philosophical post-mortem and find out what really went wrong.

The tragedy of Martin is that he died a victim of social forces which—thanks to Whitey's opium of Christianity—he did not really understand. He based his civil rights philosophy on Gandhi's Passive Resistance. But the sad truth—and it must be told—is that Martin's interpretation of Gandhism was hopelessly wrong. To put it bluntly, Martin did not understand Gandhism. And this ignorance was encour-

aged and in fact glamourised by a Whitey Establishment
which had a vested interest in Black man's self-delusion.

The first thing to know about Gandhi's Passive Resistance
is that it is not a 'minority philosophy'. The first principle
of practical Gandhism is that it is strictly a 'majority
philosophy'. By that, I mean that it is a philosophy designed
to apply only in societies where the oppressed people form
the majority of the population. How does it work? Passive
Resistance simply means that the oppressed masses who comprise the bulk of a population are organised to 'do nothing'
and, because they constitute the majority, their doing nothing brings the social machine to automatic standstill. Yet the
Establishment cannot lay their hands on anyone because you
cannot arrest someone doing nothing. That is all it means.

Understandably, therefore, Passive Resistance, unlike the
guerilla tactics, cannot be a 'minority tactic'. It simply
cannot work in a society where the oppressed people are less
in number than the oppressors. It is therefore out of place
in a country like the United States (where the oppressed
African-Americans are outnumbered by the Whitey oppressor race). Because while Blacks are out in the streets marching
and resisting peacefully and passively, the Whites are indoors
at work, keeping the social machine going and laughing their
heads off. The aim of the resistance movement, which is the
instant halting of the social machine, can never therefore
be achieved here. And anyway, it is ridiculous to apply a
philosophy which relies on effective withdrawal of labour
for its success to a situation where the very thing you are
protesting about is lack of labour. How can you withdraw
what you never had in the first place? No, Passive Resistance
in the United States is like flogging a dead horse. Mere self-
delusion.

The goal of the Passive Resistance tactic is to cripple an
unpopular Establishment by paralysing all functioning of
society by mass inaction. Its aim is to kick the power structure
in the groin by jamming the gear of all mass-dependable
national institutions. Its objective is to damage, not compromise.

Seeing it in this light, one soon discovers that Gandhi's

Passive Resistance is not a non-violent philosophy after all. On the contrary, it is one of the most violent philosophies ever devised by the human mind. What is different about it is that it does its damage unseen and that, while the enemy is lulled into the illusion of morality and peaceful intentions, the weapon of destruction is wielded so invisibly and effectively that the striking power is, on the practical level, a catastrophy. It is therefore not true to say that Gandhi got rid of violence in revolution. What he did was make violence invisible.

Resistance, even by definition, implies the use of force. How then can it be non-violent? Gandhi's Passive Resistance is simply revolutionary violence in disguise. But its destructive power only comes through the weight of numbers. If this is insufficient, it is like driving a car without an engine. Like all revolutionary philosophies, it has to be understood to be used creatively. Applied in the right situation, in a society where the victimised masses comprise the bulk of the nation, it works wonders. But misunderstood and used in the wrong social medium, it can become a dangerous boomerang which returns to slay the careless operator. Martin Luther King was a case in point. Martin's cardinal mistake was to quote Gandhi out of context. Like many Christian preachers who had been groping for years for a philosophy which would give an answer to the increasing demands of oppressed peoples for human rights without flouting the pacifism of the Christian religion, Martin jumped on Gandhism and clung to it so feverishly that he even forgot to first read the ABC of it. Mesmerised by the apparent absence of violence, he failed to see that the bloodlessness of it is not the real objective, but only incidental. The real objective of Passive Resistance, as we have described above, is instant dislocation of the Establishment. This was not what Martin was doing. He was compromising with the Establishment, integrating the oppressed African-Americans into the very social machine they were supposed to dislocate. This was a negation of Gandhism which, as we have seen, ended in disaster.

The end of Martin Luther King is the signal end of an era in African-American revolutionary thinking. His story is the sad one of a Black man who spent his whole life trying to be American and died a Black man. He was not killed for preaching Blackism like Marcus Garvey. They did not murder him for being ultra-militant like Brother Malcolm. They did not assassinate him for being an evangelist of Black Power like Brother Rap Brown who is now rotting in jail. Their reason for killing Martin was that he was a Black man. And when a man who preached love like Martin was not even exempted from the White fascist's murder list, what Black man in America can carry innocence to such a point of folly as still to believe he is safe in that racist hell of a country?

America is a violent society. It is a country where 160,000 people are maimed, killed or raped each year. In 1963 alone, more than 8,500 people were murdered, many in broad daylight on public streets, with the President of the country, John F. Kennedy, topping the list. In 1964, the FBI reported an average of 56 rapes a day across the land, a number which has become frightfully worse over the years. In New York, the 'Big Deal' capital of the Western World, the model city and the dream paradise of Western man, at least four women are raped every day and major crime is committed every three minutes. Women are obliged to take up judo to protect themselves while walking the streets and, on police advice, carry whistles to attract attention in case of attack. Good advice, too, because the figures show that 105 women in every 100,000 are liable to sexual assault. And if we remember that about 2,500,000 Americans were treated for mental illness in hospitals and clinics in 1965, of which nearly a third were classified as psychotic (a person who, by minimum definition, has lost touch with reality), it is even more terrifying to know that this figure has swollen many times today.

The first time I went to America I had only been in the country a few hours when I opened a paper and the first thing I read was that a man had strolled calmly into a nurses' apartment in Chicago and murdered eight young nurses in cold blood, inviting his victims into their death chamber one by one. A few days after that, August 12, 1966, *Time*

Magazine reported that 'on the sun-dappled mall, Mrs Claire Wilson, 18, eight months pregnant, was walking from an anthropology class when a bullet crashed into her abdomen; she survived, but later gave birth to a still-born child whose skull had been crushed by a shot. A horrified classmate, Freshman Thomas Eckman, 19, knelt beside her to help, was shot dead himself. Mathematician Robert Boyer, 33, en route to a teaching job in Liverpool, England, where his pregnant wife and two children were awaiting him, stepped out on to . . .' Yes, he too, was shot. The mass murderer, Charles Whitman, a student himself, had killed his own mother and wife, shooting 13 others and wounding 31.

Time's verdict was that 'Charles Whitman may have been unusual in having a dozen guns at his disposal, but he was by no means unique. Americans have always been a gun-toting people . . . Today the US has the world's largest civilian cache; some 100 million hand guns. Every year, more than 1,000,000 dangerous weapons are sold by mail order in the US, another million or so imported . . . The FBI reports that 57 per cent of the homicides in the US last year were committed with firearms . . .'

Time could hardly be accused of being anti-American. It is therefore interesting to read from its pages the admission that 'many psychiatrists believe that there is something intrinsic in modern American society that causes on occasion the sort of senseless mayhem practised last week in Austin. Some of the violence of the frontier still lingers in the American character, they believe, aggravated to extremes in a few individuals by the pressure to succeed and the social and economic mobility of American society.'

This is the 'civilisation' that American Presidents have sworn 'to preserve at all cost,' and are prepared to exterminate millions of Vietnamese people and topple Sukarno and Nkrumah to impose upon the unwilling Black masses of the world. This is the Americanoia, the Yankee Sambo disease, which Martin Luther King wanted to cure by 'coalition of conscience'. No wonder he called it a dream. You cannot coalise conscience with a man who has no conscience. You cannot base your revolution on morality in a world where expediency has supplanted morality. You cannot introduce a love-your-neighbour morality in a society in which the economic system is a negation of that morality. If you try, you find yourself running up the escalator of history when it is in fact going down, and the higher up you strive and sweat to get, the lower down it carries you.

Not long ago, the White man went over to the 'new world' to set up a nation modelled on Europe. And as Frantz Fanon has pointed out, he succeeded so beautifully that that society has today become the greatest lunatic asylum in the world— America. Now the White man is asking the Black man to repeat the mistake, to model his new states in Africa on medieval Anglo-Saxon customs, and to pattern his life on European tribal attitudes and decadent man-defiling social indulgences.

We say no to this because we have our own African and Asian cultural patterns which happen to be just as dear to us as the White's man's are to him. Black Power signals a rejection of all destructive White values which Whitey has been forcing down our throats ever since we came out of our mothers' wombs. And because we reject what is so patently evil and incompatible with Black personality and the revolutionary programme of the Third World, they call us 'extreme'. Because we say 'Black is Beautiful' when they have been saying 'White is Beautiful' for centuries, they call us 'racist'. Because we say that justice and peace are two different things and that we therefore prefer the former to the latter, they call us 'demagogic'. Because we distinguish ourselves from the old Black politicians who merely defended the idea of Black freedom as opposed to the Black Power revolutionary of today whose whole life is dedicated to translating that idea into reality, they call us 'irresponsible'.

Their favourite argument against Black Power is that it does not have mass Black support. But did they not use the same argument in the days of slavery? They called those slaves who demanded the cessation of slavery an 'irresponsible minority' too. They argued that the slave was better-off as a slave because then he did not have to worry about food, rent or protection. Just as they are decrying Black Power today, they decried slave freedom then as the slogan of a few agitators, a minority voice. We know better today, of course. History has taught us that while you may not judge a revolutionary movement by what the minority is saying, you must judge it by how the majority is reacting to what the minority is saying.

Black Power is here to stay and there is no force in the world that can stop us. It is a hurricane which will sweep all White sinister influences into the gutter and purify the Black world of colonialism, neo-colonialism and imperialism. It is now rocking North America like a tornado and already making significant inroads into South America. In the West Indies and Asia, its influence is growing and scaring the pants off neo-colonialist establishments. In Nigeria, a dynamic branch has been formed under the tough leadership of our indomitable brothers and sisters at the University College, Ibadan, and letters have been pouring in from all parts of Africa to bring news of many new branches under formation and growing memberships. This is magnificent because, when all is said and done, Africa is the Black Mother of Black Power, and if we let that mother be raped to death by the blue-eyed devil, we shall have been reduced to a level of cultural, political and economic orphans who, in a scramble for a sleeping place, have foolishly grabbed the mat while others have grabbed the land, to find at nightfall that we have nowhere to lay our mat.

Here in London too the Black Power movement is feared and hated like hell by the Establishment and their lackeys, who are doing everything in their power to destroy us. But they have a lot to learn.

At first they tried police brutality and intimidation, but were soon forced to slow it down when they realised that driving us underground could be to repeat the mistake of America. Then they tried using false propaganda in their papers and television to present Black Power as a meaning-less slogan and we countered by launching a manifesto which soon wiped the smile off their faces. Then they resorted to the old game of divide-and-conquer by using certain 'politi-cian' buffoons, as they did successfully in Guyana, to set

Indians against Africans and to split the movement, but they soon found that, with the exception of one or two reactionary mutts who have saved us the embarrassment of having them thrown out by leaving themselves (to start an open-air Black-and-White free-for-all tampax revolution), our movement is now, mainly because of this purge, able to move on a more responsible keel, attracting the right kind of people at long last, and able to pursue the real Black Power programme without delaying and side-tracking interference from dunder-headed Tomboes in natty dresses whose political conscience is controlled to the rattle of Whitey's cash.

Then they tried character-assassination, spreading wild and false rumours about the most-dreaded leaders of the movement, using what Brother Malcolm, from personal experience, once called Whitey's science of imagery, to defame and alienate the leadership from the masses, but they have found out too late that the natty alternatives which they have been dangling before the masses, apart from being mediocre, have a reputation known only too well to the ghetto Blacks and therefore could not defeat a fly in a popularity contest if the platform is moral responsibility.

When everything failed, they put out the tale that the Black Power movement was 'dead' simply because we decided that it was no longer necessary to go howling at Speakers' Corner every Sunday, betraying our day-to-day revolutionary development to the enemy, when the time would be better employed doing fieldwork in the ghetto where we are badly needed. Our only advice to those calling us dead is not to attempt to come to our funeral, or it might turn out to be their own.

The most dangerous weapon they have used against us is the 'critic with unsoiled hands'. These people are Black infiltrators and spies who join the movement as ultra-militants but whose only duty is to frustrate and sabotage our every constructive programme with petty criticisms and tale-carrying. We agree with Brother Robert Williams when he writes that 'criticism and self-criticism promoted from a constructive point of view is a boon to progress and success.' We agree even more when he hastily points out:

However, there is a type of critic and criticism newly arrived on the scene that the movement could do without. This new type of professional armchair critic is an expert with clairvoyant powers, he is critical of everything and most cynical in his role as a self-righteous judge with the cleanest of hands. He is a great general who has never been to battle; he understands everything but how to get involved in the struggle. To his way of thinking everything is wrong, but he has nothing better to offer. *He wants to lead the leaders* and influence the movement, but he doesn't want to suffer the penalty of leadership. He wants to have his say in the movement without casting his lot for better or worse with the daring masses. In this critic with unsoiled hands' book if a leader is not publicised by the master's press, it's because his accomplishments are not noteworthy. If a leader is given note in the boss's press, the witty critic says this is because he is loved for his latent services to the power-structure. Some of these critics are just plain soreheads, some have no knowledge of the function of the power-structure's news media and some are *outright agents planted in the ghetto to create suspicion and dissension . . .*

We must be cautious of allowing critics with unsoiled hands to force us to put all our cards on the table. We must guard against confusion cloaked in the deceptive garb of self-appointed purifiers and witch-hunters playing the part of God. Beware of the critic with unsoiled hands. His hands are the cleanest because he is not making any contribution. He has time to become a professional critic because his only error is in doing nothing. *The movement can do well without him because he is a General who leads armies only to confusion.* He is already defeated because he is motivated only by cynicism and sarcasm.

They have done, are doing, and no doubt will continue to do everything in their power to pull us down, but and by all let this be heard, we won't sway. Like Martin, we too have been to the mountain top, but, unlike him, we see blood in the distance flowing like a million Nigers in scarlet.

We can see White men in the next decade knocking and asking in broken Swahili for social integration; and we can hear the Black militia guarding the gates of the Iroko Curtain around Black Africa replying that Whitey's Swahili is not yet good enough. We can also hear the voices of our children swearing before the shrine of our thick-lipped, flat-nosed, ebony-black God of Beauty saying:

'The blood of our fathers has flowed to wash away our blindness and given us sight to see you as you really are, O Black God of Beauty. We are sons and daughters of MEN who died young in battle because they did not live on their knees. Give us courage to sustain this greatest heritage so costly won.

Black Power or Death!'

Kangaroo in My Soul

(Written when I was Editor of Black Power Speaks)

ONE OF the greatest drawbacks to Black realisation of full manhood today is the pale kangaroo within the soul of the Black man. 'Burn, baby, burn' has become the Black war-cry of late, but how many of us Blacks have realised that we must first of all burn the White man within ourselves?

We all want a change of conditions, but how many of us have observed that we ourselves are part of these conditions?

One of the tragic consequences of colonialism is that every Black man in the world today has two psychologically antagonistic individuals existing within himself, one White, one Black. And whether someone is Uncle Tom or Black revolutionary depends on which one of these two personalities is dominating the other. In most cases, unfortunately, it is the White one that is ruthlessly dominating the Black.

The result is what we call *intrapersonal colonialism*, which means that, even within oneself, a curious sort of hidden and unconscious colonialism is going on, in which the White man inside us is still domineering over the Black man. This is soul colonialism, the worst type of colonialism because— thanks largely to Anglo-Saxon education—it thrives on the passivity of its victim.

Black Power demands a total rejection of Whiteyism, without or within. To talk Black Power, we must first clear up the mess inside our soul. Before we can effectively reject Whiteyism in the street, we must first and foremost reject it within the very marrow of our beings. It must be rejected because it has no right to be there.

It has no right to be there because it is a bastard of imperialism. What put it there is not a legitimate social process, but a colonial artificial insemination calculated to bastardise our mentality, mutilate our personality, and make us intellectual hybrids whose sense of loyalty is so split and confused that we can no longer think or fend for ourselves.

We must abort this White man within us because getting

46

rid of him is the only cure for the gnawing schizophrenia colonialism has instilled into us. We accept that rejecting the Whitey in yourself is more difficult than rejecting Whitey-ism in the street because it means rejecting a part of yourself, or to put it more correctly, it means asking you to destroy what you have always believed to be part of yourself.

Nevertheless it must be done. It is the first stage in Black Power revolutionary development. As we have pointed out above, it is impossible to reject the devil of Whiteyism out in the street when there is a Whitey in your soul sympathising with his kin in the street.

Rejecting Whiteyism in the street is only the last stage of the struggle. Because when it comes to this last stage, it is the Black man who will be acting, not a man who is half Black and half White. But because some of the Black 'leaders' today see the Black revolution as mere over-night self-transmutation into Rap Browns, Che Guevaras and Ho Chi Mins, they have concentrated so much on the last stage of the struggle that they have completely lost sight of the first and more vital character-seasoning stage of it.

They have failed to see that revolutionary consciousness is only a product of an attained state of mind and that we cannot become Rap Browns until we have unwrapped the White mantle colonialism has wrapped round our psyche.

There are some of our Caribbean brothers who shout Black Power with all genuineness but are embarrassed every time they run into an African in national dress. Some have been known to skip one train compartment for another just to avoid being identified with some group of robed Africans speaking in Yoruba or Swahili.

'Why don't those bloody Africans lower their voices for Christ's sake?' some of them swear angrily. But what they are actually saying is that the Black tongue is so shameful that, if it must be spoken at all, it must be spoken in whispers and so apologetically that it does not offend the ears of the good White master race.

And the shame of it is that the very Black man who hates to hear 'Africans' speak Yoruba is always the first to pop his eyes out in rapture at a group of long-clawed au pair girls shouting French at the top of their voices.

This, however, is not wholly his fault. What is happening here is that the White man within ourselves has come to colonise and dominate the Black half of our individuality so uncompromisingly that the very sight of African dress or the sound of an African language strikes us as a threat to our survival and affects us as a reminder of that Black part of ourselves we are subconsciously trying to forget.

It is the Whitey in us rejecting and spitting at Black values and culture all over again.

When a Black woman puts on a wig or burns her hair to 'whiten' her exterior, it is the Whitey inside her person struggling for exterior representation after interior domination.

When a Black man from Barbados is at pains to point out, even casually to an 'African' lighter in complexion than himself, that he is a European because his great grandmother once went to bed with an Irish sailor two months after she was already pregnant with his grandfather, it is once again the White kangaroo in the Black man manifesting itself in a sinister manner.

On the other hand, there are some of our 'African' brothers, mostly from West Africa, who shout African Personality at the top of their voices, and with all sincerity too, but will have nothing to do with a West Indian worker in Brixton who does not speak with a Higgins-perfect English accent.

Some have been known to shun a party of straw-hatted West Indians speaking 'un-English English', and what's more not wearing starched white collars, spotted Inns-of-Court ties, and three-piece suits.

They will defend Pan-Africanism with every long word in the dictionary and turn round the next minute to wink at their English girl friends the moment a West Indian 'Ndi Ogede' worker passes them by, and then proceed to explain, in a desperate attempt to dispel embarrassment, that 'these West Indians cause all the trouble in this country because they lower the standards.'

Whose standards? The White standards of course which

the Whitey in our soul is fighting desperately to preserve.

Let's face it, brother, we have got it bad. These are facts about ourselves which we must face before we can move another inch. If not, we will be building a Black freedom edifice on mere sand.

It follows that 'Burn, baby, burn' must begin with the burning of that cancerous Whitey in ourselves. The first move towards Black consciousness is to kill that part of yourself that is White. The number one step towards Black Power orientation is to commit partial suicide.

It is necessary and healthy suicide. It is an internal baptism of fire which must consume the White devil in the core of our personality, to free the Black half of our ego, which is the real us, to develop and fill the entire wholeness of our being.

The first casualty in the Black and White confrontation must be the White infiltrator in our soul. The enemy within must die before we can face the enemy without. We must be in complete command of our fortress before we can venture to carry the battle beyond the walls of our being.

To do things for ourselves, we must first make sure we are completely ourselves. Before we can say WE confidently, we must first ascertain we really mean WE, not half-US, half-THEM.

Contrary to what some of us have been misled by the White press to think, Black Power is not just an idea we advocate to frighten the Whites. It is a very personal thing like religion and begins with a deep personal conviction that the 'White man is dead' within ourselves and that, from the day of our resolve onwards, we are wholly Black.

On the practical level, it is the way you live, what you wear, how you walk, what you read, how you think, what you eat, how you comport yourself, what language you speak . . . in short, a way of life. We don't want to be misunderstood. We reject pure cultural nationalism which has no political or ideological orientation. It is almost as dangerous as its extreme opposite—doctrinaire infantile Leftism which, owing to sudden exposure to abstract Marxism, is yet uninformed about the paramount relationship between economics and culture, and has yet to learn that colonialism has been triumphant largely because the culture of the colonial countries has been successfully transformed into a commodity for sale, exchangeable with the raw materials of Africa and other colonised countries of the world.

We read a lot about the 'riots' and violence going on in America. But there is an aspect of that struggle that the White press has, for obvious reasons, underplayed and, in most cases, suppressed. And that is the raging Black consciousness which is the bedrock upon which the Afro-American rebellion is based. Let the following extract from Earl Caldwell's article in the *International Herald Tribune* of Monday, March 18, 1968, speak for itself:

Along the littered blocks of Seventh Avenue in Central Harlem, the little African shops stick out among the steamy restaurants, the noisy bars and the drab tenements. There was a time when the shops might have appeared out of place in Harlem. But not today. 'More and more', a resident of Harlem explained, 'the black man here is moving toward an African frame of mind.'

In the strip along Seventh Avenue between 116th and 135th Street, there are four African boutiques, offering items ranging from wood carvings and hand-made earrings to paintings and native dress. But the surge in African influence is not confined to the shops alone.

On the streets women stroll about in long, bright-coloured African dress. And young men wear danshikis and bubas, colourful jacket-like African shirts. Ask a dark, bearded young man on the street what it means and he answers: 'It means that the black man is progressing. We're getting away from that European bag.'

Not everyone uptown is being touched by the African influence but it is growing. Parents have taken to giving their children African names. At night, groups of adults hurry off to attend lectures on African culture. Entire families have enrolled in African language courses at the Olatunji Centre for African Culture.

In the schools now there are displays on Negro history

and signs that read 'Black is Beautiful'. At Taft High School in the Bronx, one African language, Swahili, is now being offered and there are plans to include the course next year at a number of other schools. Among the adults, some small groups have sought out African religions and observe them regularly now in colourful services that include religious dances and songs . . .

This is Black America today. It is Black Power in action. It is the spirit sweeping across the Afro-American world like a raging wind.

When Stokely Carmichael was in Africa recently, he told the people of Tanzania that the African-Americans have now adopted Swahili as their 'national' language in America. And when he returned to the States, he married the lovely Miriam Makeba. This is what Black Power within a mature ideological setting means to Stokely Carmichael, Rap Brown and other militant Black leaders in the States.

It means not only the cry 'Burn, baby, burn' but, above all, what tongue you speak and the choice of the mother of your children.

Compare this with what is happening back home in Africa, which should be the home and Black mother of Black Power. Reactionary 'leaders' are busy aping the White men and shamelessly bleaching the African personality. They have been to England to be taught how the British constitution is unwritten and gone away not realising that it has been indelibly engraved on their mentalities.

They have returned to their home lands to lower the Union Jack while presiding over the Independence ceremony in academic gowns made from a more conservative shade of the Union Jack.

While Kamuzu Banda is trotting the streets of Europe in a bowler hat, speaking and being English in England and Welsh in Wales, he still refuses to see the folly, the immorality, and the short-sightedness of his economic love-ins with Southern African White fascists who would rather die than speak and be 'African' in Africa.

Compare the American Black scene with what is going

on here in Britain. The nattiest dressed men in London are found among the Black 'leaders' and 'revolutionaries'. Some never make a public appearance unless they are in three-piece suits, with watch chains dangling across front waist-coat pockets, and a glint of regret in their eyes that the monocle is no longer in use.

Some Black 'revolutionary' orators have not infrequently told White hecklers at Hyde Park's Speakers Corner: 'I am better than you. Look at you. And look at my suit. I am better dressed than you.' And the typical response is thunderous applause by the Black section of the crowd. Surely this is wrong. How can you decry a man for being evil and at the same time employ his standards to evaluate yourself?

It is this type of plain-speaking that makes the Black Power movement enemies, I know. But the truth must be told. It is far better to antagonise a brother than let him be a friend and wallow in self-delusion, especially when his self-delusion is a drawback and an embarrassment to international Black revolution.

One of the 'crimes' we have been accused of by these 'revolutionaries' was trying to start a Black Power School of Culture where the Black peoples of Britain could come to learn Swahili, Hindi, the History of the Third World, Guerrilla tactics, Self-defence, Judo, etc. In fact, one 'revolutionary' declared indignantly, while opposing the scheme, that he was no African and didn't give a damn about African culture. He has since become an avowed enemy of the Black Power movement.

We do not wish to deny these men the right to call themselves 'revolutionary'. After all, the term 'revolutionary' has become rather elastic of late, particularly in Britain. What we do stress strongly, however, and most emphatically, is that such men, whatever they are or choose to call themselves, are not Black Power in orientation or motivation and will do well to adjust or piss off.

We have not said either, and do not say, that the aim of the Black Power movement is to make people put on African clothes, period! We do say, however, that Black cultural nationalism, as exampled by the wearing of African robes in Harlem, is a manifestation of a mental attitude called Black Power consciousness. In other words, Black Power is a state of mind. A degree of conviction or committedness to Blackness.

It means being sufficiently proud of being Black to see the White attack on the collective Black personality as a personal attack; an attack which must be staved off at all costs.

It is upon this spiritual bedrock that the Black revolution must be based. Without it, one might find out too late that the readiness to die for the cause is not there. One only dies for a cause when one is the cause; and sees every attack on that cause as an attack on one's own person or as the assault of a loved one. Violence can only result from this state of mind.

Some of us have often wondered what made men like Marcus Garvey (the great leader of the Back to Africa campaign in the States) tick. To say that they were born heroic messiahs is a myth. The simple explanation is that by a curious combination of circumstances, like reading a book, or meeting someone, or even reading about someone as Malcolm X did about Elija Muhammad in prison, they began to enquire and, through dedication, get at the truth and reach a degree of personal conviction to accept that Whitey in their soul deserved to die.

And killing this Whitey, they felt a new degree of confidence in themselves so that, even at the risk of death, they went out to redeem the souls of their Black contemporaries.

What distinguished them from their contemporaries was the degree of Black consciousness in their souls.

Yes, Marcus Garvey developed as a state of mind, Malcolm X was also a state of mind. Stokely Carmichael is a state of mind. Black Power is a state of mind. It is very easy to attain. The simple thing to do is to kill that capitalist pale kangaroo hugging the core of your soul.

According to the Old Man of China, before you can put something into a man's hand you must first put something into his head. And to become invincible we must first become invisible. That is what this essay is about.

POSTSCRIPT

Pure cultural nationalism must be deplored, yes. But we must also guard against neo-Uncle-Tom-ism, the philosophy of neo-We-shall-overcome-ism, based on abstract internationalism and infantile Lefticism which, in the long run, is the most dangerous enemy to the practical realisation of true Marxist revolution all over the world, and particularly in the Third World countries that are dialectically poised to spark off that revolution. We must not allow ourselves to be goaded by the false flatteries of false friends into a situation where we, as unconscious neo-Toms, are doing more harm to the revolution than the cultural nationalists we so piously condemn.

The Little Boy of Brussels

(First of the essays written in prison)

LAST NIGHT a little Black boy was brought into prison, convicted on a drug charge. He looked hardly seventeen and was very frightened as he was marched away from the reception block. You could tell he was feeling homesick already and was probably thinking of his mother.

We, prisoners of A Wing, were on the lawn outside, having our evening exercise at the time. The boy looked completely lost and bewildered. But as he glanced in our direction, he suddenly fixed his eyes on me and smiled. In that fraction of a second, his timidity seemed to have vanished and I could see that he was pleasantly surprised to find a familiar face here. I could not recollect having met or seen him before but I did not dwell on that too long. All that was important was that, wherever he had seen me before, recognising me here again as a Black friend in this pale sea of pale faces was edifying to his young nerves. I felt good inside, smiled back, and winked at him. His shy sweet smile broadened into a merry grin and his white teeth sparkled like Azanian pearls against the lovely and smooth duskiness of his face. He was almost ecstatic. A really delighted child!

But just then, the White prison officer who was marching him away caught him with this grin on his face. The officer looked round, wondering what the boy was smiling at. At that point, a White lady doctor of about fifty was ascending the steps of the nearby Prison Hospital. And without any shadow of doubt in his mind, the prison officer decided that it was this White woman that the Black boy was smiling at. The warder's face registered a sadistic rage. And pulling the boy by the ear, the warder jerked his head forward and backward, spitting out a staccato of swear-words in between warnings that if the boy did not keep his eyes off White women, next time he would be put away for life. When the boy tried to protest, though only feebly, the warder only got angrier and booted him in the arse. And still swearing, he

55

marched the boy away towards F Wing. The poor frightened little boy didn't dare look back at me again.

'Keep walking, Bro,' I heard a voice say behind me and felt a brotherly hand on my shoulder. I didn't realise I had stopped. I turned. It was Biado Lawal, a one-eyed Guyanese prison veteran who had lost his right eye in a skirmish with screws some years back, and had adopted his African name from sheer desperation to clutch at some semblance of his Black identity in White-prison surroundings that have, over the years, been systematically whittling away his individuality. He was my mentor on racial attitudes in British prisons —and he knew the lot inside out. 'Play cool, Bro,' he added consolingly, squeezing me on the shoulder. 'You ain't seen nothing yet.'

But for me, that was enough. A Black boy of almost minor age! A mere child! And a White woman old enough to be his Great Grannie! He didn't even know she was there, let alone smile at her in lust! But the white prison screw was quite satisfied that this nigger-boy untouchable desired this lily-white paragon of womanhood. And must be booted in the arse for it.

Biado told me later that Black prisoners convicted of 'White rape' were the most brutalised of prisoners in any jail, even more so than political 'trouble-makers' like me. And I could well understand it.

For, when all is said and done, sex is what 'Negrophobia' is all about. The White man believes that the Black man's idea of happiness is the White woman, that the Black man's dream of heaven and self-elevation is diving into White flesh, that every Black man on this earth is after White women and does nothing all day and night but think and dream of how to get one in bed; and then goes berserk with desire the moment any White object in a skirt comes along. Which shows how woefully ignorant of the Black man the White man is.

In the first place, the relationship between the White woman and the Black man is not a normal one. It is hardly a relationship capable of inducing 'love' in the normal man-woman sense of the word. Love is not possible between them.

Ironical as it may sound, the fact remains that no Black man ever makes 'love' to a White woman he does not despise. When a Black man is in bed with a White woman, he is not looking for pleasure. He is seeking revenge. He sees the White woman, not as a woman, but as a piece of England or any other White nation that has rampaged over his fatherland. He sees the White woman as a unit of the Caucasianism that for centuries has held Black manhood bound. He sees himself as living proof of the one-sided exploitation of human resources in which the Whites have become men at the expense of the Blacks. The White man has attained manhood by devaluing Black manhood, culturally, politically, economically. In the West, this devaluation progression has been from the 'Black' to the 'Negro', and back home in Africa, from Chiaka and Chetewayo to Tshombe.

The White woman therefore represents the mascot of the White male plunderer, the recipient of the looted booty, the bitch behind the throne of napalm and bayonets. Every piece of jewelry that glitters on her neck has a history of unrewarded Black toil, sweat and blood behind it. And that blood is still flowing today.

Her mascot value apart, the White woman represents the refined and delicate embodiment of White 'civilisation' and what is beautiful in it. She is also the vehicle for the White oppressors and soldiers of tomorrow, the future threats to the Black manhood of our children and children's children. Above all, she is the one thing that the White soldiers and rapists of Black women hold sacred . . . or at least pretend to. Besides, she is approachable and vulnerable.

This makes her, to the Black man, the target of Black vengeance. As a symbol of European motherhood, she deserves to be raped. As a 'forbidden fruit' of the master, she has to be eaten. As a personification of all that is deemed beautiful in Caucasianism, she deserves to be destroyed.

That is why the Black man in bed with a White woman behaves like a destroyer. Every time a White woman undresses and lies down in pose to receive him, it is imperialism yawning in front of him. (As if it hasn't swallowed enough!) Consciously or unconsciously, he is out to blast the hell out of what he considers two fleshy slices of ever-greedy colonialism. He ceases to be a 'dog' Uncle-Tommishly wagging his 'tail' in joy and becomes a 'cat' and then the wagging of the 'tail' of erection is no longer in servile welcome but in grim vengeful dictatorship. His every up-and-down motion becomes motivated by hate and, like the piston of a roaring locomotive, he descends on her every time like a hammer. He is not making love to her; he is giving her a beating. He knows in his heart he could get just as much satisfaction from slapping her face as he does from sleeping with her but, after what he has suffered, it is more fun hitting a mean enemy literally below the belt. And what he discharges in the process is not the milk of overflowing love, but time-chalked droppings of Black venom. That is why he feels the opposite of what he might be supposed to. A Black man on top of a White woman is a guerrilla activist, gyrating to kill.

The tragedy of the White woman, however, is that she mistakes this guerrilla offensive for expertise. With tears she acclaims her Black assailant as the greatest of lovers and reveres the Black race as the most passionate of races.

What she does not realise is that every sex experience she has with a Black man is a narrow escape from murder. She doesn't know, poor thing, that every groan she utters during a sex act is sweet music to his Black ears, real balm on the soul of her Black 'lover'. What she sees in the eyes of her Black 'expert' is not the fire of loving passion but the blaze of hatred that has long smouldered. She fails to realise that the Black 'lover' tears her apart in bed because he wants to tear her apart literally, from limb to limb, not to kill her outright, because, once dead, your enemy is beyond pain. Having torn her apart just sufficiently to keep her panting for breath, he then begins to crack his 'whip' on her in the very anatomical vicinity where her White ancestors, not so long ago, lashed his Black forebears as slaves. Every downward thrust into her is like a slashing-in of an assegai into the White marrow of her being. And every withdrawal is a preparation for another attack.

This is no sex. It is a protest. A practical protest against cohabitation with her. It is like a girl biting a male attacker (during a rape assault) on his lips angrily to show she does not want to bite the very same lips lovingly in a sexual kiss. It is counter-sex, a sort of spitting at what is found repulsive; it is frigidity masquerading as activity in order to denigrate. The Black man cannot make 'love' 'passionately' to the White woman unless he despises her intensely. In short, the celebrated Black man's flesh-craziness for White women is, after all, a declaration of war. War against imperialism in the flesh. War on the White despoiler of dark races. War on White domination. I do not pretend that every man with a black skin reacts this way to White women. This would be too sweeping a generalisation. The reaction I describe is what distinguishes the Black man from the Negro. It is not always conscious either. Because it is not an attitude. When a man strikes you and you strike him back, that's not an attitude, it's instinct. Despite the fact that many of us would hate to admit it, it is there nevertheless and remains the only rational explanation for the abnormal 'attraction' of the Black man to the White woman.

Dr Martin Luther King, just before his assassination, declared that riots were the voice of the unheard. In the same vein, the Black man's genitals have become the weapon of the unarmed.

We must pursue this analysis to its logical conclusion. The Black man will only stop 'fighting' the White woman the day he gets himself a weapon to fight the White man. The Black man can only stop finding the White woman 'irresistible' the day he learns to find the gun more 'attractive'. He will forget his White mistress the night he learns to hug the gun-powder Teddy bear. He can only ignore the White shrew when he decides to tame the White shrew-maker master who is oppressing both the White shrew and himself. There is no other way.

That the Black man is superior in bed is a myth. That he performs differently with a White woman in bed is a fact. But this difference is not a reflection of any high degree of skill emanating from any racial idiosyncrasy. It reflects only the frustration of the oppressed Black man nibbling violently at the mother of his White oppressors of tomorrow with the only instrument at his disposal.

But the White woman, knowing no better, sticks to her story. And the White man, knowing even less, believes this myth and suffers from a perennially-gnawing xenophobic inferiority complex. And some Black men, desirous of being 'superior' at something, even if it is only fornication, take on the role of testicle-carriers whose only significance in society lies in the potentiality of their genitals and, sublimating away the energy they need to squeeze the trigger in screwing White women, they remain perpetual hewers of wood, fetchers of water and, to use the expression Sparrow made famous, waterers of White gardens.

Is it any wonder that the one and only image of Black manhood immortalised in monument in the grottoes of Western Europe is in the pose of the Little Boy of Brussels?

Letter from Brixton Prison

DEAR DOLORES,

I feel like writing you this letter because I am in remand-custody in Brixton Prison and don't know what will become of me tomorrow. You have every right to rip it up, if you like, without reading a word. Had you done so already, I wouldn't hold it against you. But since you have started reading, I will presume you want to know what made me behave the way I did. I will therefore waste no time praising your nobility of spirit. To do so at this stage could easily be misconstrued as condescending and therefore fatal. But one thing you must know right away is that you are the most beautiful eighteen-year-old woman I have ever seen in the nude. This makes my action even more difficult to explain, but, unless you have this fact from the start, there can be no further dialogue between us. Unless you believe that what I did had nothing to do with any physical or moral inadequacy you might think you have, we cannot proceed. And we have to proceed, if not for your sake, for mine. We mustn't let them see our tears, must we, Dolores?

It was not until you ran out of the hotel room that night that the full implication of my action came crashing in on me. I suppose, had there been a third witness, this might sound an exaggeration, especially as you walked quite slowly out of the room, your head bowed, tears running down your face, your dazed figure dragging like a little girl some priest had refused absolution after her first confession. I watched you till the door closed noiselessly behind you. It was a quiet and unhurried retreat, but you and I know—as you alone knew then—that you were running as fast as your laden heart would let you. It was not until later, much, much, later, that it dawned on me what agony you were living through. And I wouldn't have known it but for the echo of your last words.

'I am sorry I have only succeeded in making you feel this

61

way. I was only trying to be a good prostitute.'

I tried to recollect how it all began. When I first set eyes on your face, I had recognised there what I had seen a thousand times before. I had seen it in the ghettoes of Washington and San Francisco, I had encountered it in Vine City, Watts and Chicago, I had witnessed it in Harlem, England's Brixton and Perry Bar. I first knew it in Port Harcourt, and later on, in Lagos and Senegal's Dakar. It exists in any corner of this earth where the pedlars of democracy have emancipated Black women to the level of peddling sex for a living. I call it the voidness of Ego or the baptism of filth. They made you wear a mask, too tightly, too long. You had been playing a part all these years, so that even you had come to believe that that part was indeed you. They had made you sell your body for a living and, to forestall your only refuge, told you you were a 'sinner' and therefore had no soul. They had called you 'Miss Shame' and you had responded, 'We sure is.'

This was what you were when we met, a self-confessing Miss Shame. And yet, within the two hours that led to that dreadful last moment, I watched you undergo a transition. The real you came out. It showed in your conversation, your laughter, your curiosities. You told me to hell with twenty dollars, with my writer's philosophies, to hell with God. Happiness glowed in your eyes as you danced around the room like a manumitted slave. I was flattered no end that I had something to do with your new-found freedom. I know I dismissed it as nothing at the time, but I was quite moved when you thanked me rather lavishly for being kind to you. I tried in vain to convince you that I was not being kind to you, period! That I meant every word I muttered.

Your two companions, the two white girls who were with you when we met, were no match for you in any way. They knew it, too, and their brashness, I thought, was a wasted attempt, a desperate one, to contradict this fact.

I was irritated at the way the one you called Barbara had accosted me on the pavement as I stepped out of my hotel. Yes, I stay here, I replied. Yes, I am foreign, African, visiting from London. No, I am not a student. No, I do not want a woman, I want some chicken. Yes, at this time of the night I happen to be starving. Yes, yes, no, no, yes! She kept on and on and on. I don't quite know whether I did it to slight her, or because I was beginning to find the curious mixture of beauty, coyness and silence that was you more and more intriguing; but, if you remember, it was at this point that I shut her up by telling her I had changed my mind.

'Didn't someone say,' I joked, 'that a woman is like a chicken? Kill her and she supplies you with nourishment.' But Barbara did not laugh when I ended up with 'I most certainly do want a woman. That one!' And I pointed at you.

Poor Barbara! She was absolutely disgusted with me. Cautioning me that you were going to cost me twenty dollars, she turned to you with that patronising air of hers to remind you that you were expected to come straight back to the joint as soon as you finished with me—evidently you were supposed to account for every twenty-dollar earning you made to appease some Rachman of the sex world.

Left alone with you, I was at my wit's end what to do with you. You must have noticed my hesitation about rushing you straight into my hotel room just to have a twenty-dollar affair. I was grateful when you came to my aid by intimating you knew of a nearby restaurant which stayed open till dawn and where the chicken was good.

The summer night was cool and enchanting, but the wind moaned ominously as we walked down 48th Street. From halting exchanges, our conversation became speedier and less inhibited. We warmed up to each other so rapidly that by the time we got to my hotel apartment and finished our packed meal, you had told me all about your unhappy childhood, your mother's tragic death and your miraculous existence. You told me more than enough to make even the most hard-hearted of men fall down and weep. Yet I did not weep, not because I am a man of strength, but because internal injuries my heart suffered from your sad retrospections were soon soothed by the sweet iodine of joy which your new animation sprayed into my soul.

I felt uncommonly edified as I watched you undergo this self-induced process of ego-manumission. Like a flower at the dawn of spring, the real you unfolded and blossomed before my eyes. You became as free as air, having decided to forget, at least for the night, that even the North wind is still amenable to the laws of the North.

It was no longer the self-abnegating Miss Shame who now looked me straight in the eyes and smiled as if challenging my manhood to stand and live up to its task. Gone were your mask, your shackles, your veil. You had not a care in the wide world when you tilted your head to one side and asked me to take you in my arms and treat you like a woman. As you said so, you looked as if, all through your life, you had been starved of all uncommercialised love. Kindness had been a foreign quantity till now and sex only a torturous gyration of the lower abdomen till twenty-dollars worth of animal friction had been cranked out of you by some inconsiderate blood-sucker, Black or White.

But today, tonight, this moment, your appetite for the first time in years, perhaps in life, was whetted, and all the feminine biological urges in you, hitherto dormant, were yearning for real masculine caresses. I understood your torment, and the necessity to complete what I had started struck me as urgent and logical.

At the time I gave you an encouraging nod, I was perfectly satisfied that all would be well. I watched you undress, watched you reveal, with every strip, that my imagination had not exaggerated the beauty of your nudity. In his poem 'The Black Woman' Marcus Garvey articulated his veneration for the beauty of Black women. As I looked at you, I felt as if a voice were whispering Garvey's words inside me.

Black queen of beauty, thou hast given color to the world!
Among other women thou art royal and the fairest!
Like the brightest jewels in the regal diadem,
Shin'st thou, Goddess of Africa, Nature's purest emblem!

Black men worship at thy virginal shrine of purest love,
Because in thine eyes are virtue's steady and holy mark,
As we see no other, clothed in silk or fine linen,
From ancient Venus, the Goddess, to mythical Helen.

The more I looked at you, the more my heart was ravished

at the sight. When you bent down to tug at the lace of my shoe, I saw the line of your neck and the curves of your rear, and immediately I became drunk in your presence. Within me, masculinity panted away like a locomotive. The flesh of your breasts and thighs was dark and lovely as the night. I felt a certain desire to press close, to caress and love you till all your tantalising pliability was exhausted. I heard myself echoing your words, 'To hell with twenty dollars, to hell with caution, to hell with God!'—

It was then that I began to undo my shirt. But, as you well know, I had only progressed as far down as the third button when my hands stilled. Something seemed to have snapped within me as I stood there, silent, gazing unseeingly over your shoulders into space. Judging by reels upon reels of thoughts and ideas that raced through my mind, I must have been in that pensive posture for a long time. The next thing I was conscious of was your voice asking me if anything was the matter. And as I replied, my voice, though sounding as if it came from afar, was a very determined voice indeed.

'Put on your clothes, Dolores.'

'What was that?'

'I said: put on your clothes.'

'But—'

'Please don't argue with me. Just do as I tell you.'

'If it is my friends you are still worried about, I told you not to bother. They can wait at the joint. I can handle them. Honest!'

'No, Dolores, I am not worried about your friends.'

'Then it must be the twenty dollars. Don't you believe me? I don't want a dime from you.'

'I know you don't. And I am flattered. But you must dress now. I am sorry.'

'Don't you understand, I feel—' You broke off, held me close and began to stroke my neck. But your hands, a moment ago radiant with the heat of passion, had suddenly become as cool and impersonal to me as a barber's touch. Female intuition! You sensed how I felt.

'I see,' you said despondently, relaxing your hold. You remained speechless and motionless, and that old mask began

E

to take hold of your countenance all over again. You tried to hold back your tears, but a shiny drop fell to the floor. You apologised for soiling my carpet and then turned to put on your clothes.

Not long afterwards, you were gone. But not before you had made a brief halt at the door to sob those last unforgetable words.

'I am sorry I have only succeeded in making you feel this way. I was only trying to be a good prostitute.'

I have stated more than once that it wasn't till minutes after you had left the wretched room that the full meaning of those words became clear to me. It was evident you had misunderstood me and misinterpreted my action. No doubt, you had taken me for a snob, a hypocrite who, in spite of my sweet words and superficial gloss, remained, when it came to the test, a westernised Tom who would not share love with one of my own kind because I considered her morally untouchable, a pariah.

With words of seeming kindness, I had encouraged you all along to break out of the social latrine (to which you were at least partially resigned) and to cultivate self-respect, to stop being a twenty-five-hour-a-day harlot, a Miss Shame with a past, and to see yourself as a young woman with a future and an ability to give and receive genuine love. But when, in spite of yourself, you began to react positively to my sweet sermons, and, indeed, the woman in you began to respond to the man before you with love that was far from illicit, I, the great preacher, could not bring myself to forget that you were a harlot. Seeing kindness and pity shining in my eyes, your keen imagination had approximated them to genuine respect and desire even to the point of love.

You offered to warm my soul with your body and, if necessary, wipe my feet with your hair. Only a woman in love could make such an offer to the man she loves. By flaunting that offer, I had proved that the only sensation I sought from your company was a titillation of ego which emanated from the contrast between your social position and mine. Whitey-defined social position!

These reflections saddened my soul. What made it most

intolerable was not so much that you had thought me worse than I deserved, but the realisation that, if I let you run away with these wrong impressions, if I did nothing immediately to correct these odious notions, I had created more psychological problems for both of us than I had set out to remedy, considering your exceedingly sensitive nature. In a matter of seconds, I was resolved.

I buttoned my shirt and dashed out of the room in the hope of catching you before you went very far. When I got to the lift-stand, you had gone. What's more, all the elevators were in use. Waiting was out of the question. I ran down the steps, all the way from the seventh to the ground floor. People in the lobby looked at me askance as I jostled through them like a madman. I ran into the street and searched everywhere. In vain. You must have taken to your heels the moment you found yourself at the other side of the door.

In desperation, I hurried down to the end of 48th Street, looked left into Times Square and right towards 49th Street. It was no use. You had disappeared. It was one of the most painful moments of my life. The more my mind dwelt on it, the more terrible I felt. I realised how stupid of me it was to presume that you would understand! And how silly to attribute the tears coursing down your cheeks to a gesture of sympathy with what was going on inside my head! And how can a girl fathom the mechanics of a strange mind? You hardly knew me! To misconstrue my motive was the most natural thing for any girl to do under those circumstances. And that was precisely what you did. Your reaction suggested it and your words revealed how soul-scathing it must have been for you.

My first impulse was to trace you to the address you gave me. I had to see you, if only to take back the dagger I had so unwittingly plunged into your bleeding heart. However, after I reflected on what you had told me about your 'landlord' and the ethics of your profession, I decided to forget it. But I made myself a promise there and then: to write you this letter as soon as I got back to London. This, Dolores, is a fulfilment of that promise.

But, having decided to write, I am beginning to realise

that the task is not as easy as I thought. To explain why I could not go to bed with you, I must first recount the last-moment thoughts which led to that resolution. To make you fathom the intensity of those thoughts, I must go back to my actual experiences in America, experiences that provoked the thoughts. And to help you appreciate my reaction to American society, it will be necessary to show you how history has moulded my reaction to the world. This means, of course, relating why I came to America, what I make of America and what America has made of me.

This therefore is my task: to dissect the America that I saw, re-define the me that you met, and show you how you came to represent a culmination of a phalanx of historical forces which have been in operation since long before our time. Having done this, I shall leave it to you to assess the wisdom or the inevitability of my action. I am under no illusion however that, given the same circumstances, stronger men than I could not have handled the situation more impressively than I did. I must therefore ask you to bear in mind that, not withstanding those romantic pictures you painted about me, you are dealing with no superman. You must remember that it is me, and what history has made of you and me, that you are judging, not a man in a vacuum.

As for me, I am strictly what the times have made me. My English education has turned me into a tramp. Education, I was once led to believe, is like a slot machine; you insert a child at the age of five and extract him fifteen years later to find him well-educated, sure of himself, and free. The machine seemed to have broken down when my turn came. The conflict between what I expected to find in England— the White man's land where the machine is designed—and what I actually saw there has since driven me into a perpetual search for the truth. My lot has become tramping about the world, seeing things and people, sharing their dreams and nightmares, writing down my findings and, one day, laying me down and dying.

It was in this spirit that I flew to America from London. I had embarked upon a journey which was to take me thousands of miles over the 'New World'.

For nearly two thousand years, European civilisation has been based on the unhealthiest of social contradictions, that between a philosophy and religion which proclaim the brotherhood of man, and an economic structure which divides mankind into masters and slaves, exploiters and exploited, victimisers and victims. America, today, represents the epitome of this social misgrowth. The experiences of Greece, Rome and Great Britain notwithstanding, the United States of America insists on championing the cause of this contradiction inherited from Europe, even if it means the destruction of mankind. Writes Dr W. E. B. Du Bois in *The Battle of Europe:*

The civilization by which America insists on measuring us and to which we must conform our natural tastes and inclinations is the daughter of that European civilization which is now rushing furiously to its doom. This civilization with its aeroplanes and submarines, its wireless and its 'big business' is no more static than that of those other civilizations in the rarest days of Greece and Rome. Behind all this gloss of culture and wealth and religion has been lurking the world-old lust for bloodshed and power gained at the cost of honour.

My first confrontation with militant Black youths was in Atlanta's SNCC Head Office, an unfurnished, dilapidated grey building in the stenchy slums of Vine City.

I saw them in their police-scaring revolutionary outfits, jeans, threadbare old clothes and overalls, as they worked from dawn till midnight, or often into the early hours of the morning. They were mostly young people, some just out of college with impressive degrees, a good many still in school, a few who simply left school because the White man taught them nothing there which could improve the plight of the Blacks. Their spirit of dedication, hard work and organisation was incredible. With the possible exception of Messenger Elijah Mohammad's Muslim Mosque in Chicago, I cannot recall anywhere else in the world having come across such a tantalising collection of beautiful Black women, all without exception wearing their hair in the 'Natural Look'.

They told me the secret of their beauty. Hard work.

We discussed Black grievances as we toured the offices. The Negro, they pointed out, is physically separated from the Whites in the United States. What the Blacks now want is a psychological separation which will allow the Whites to destroy themselves. Harlem is more compatible with Mozambique in Africa than with any White community in the States. SNCC has been striving for Black political power in areas which are predominantly Negro, but this has been frustrated by Whites. 1965 Arkansas was a case in point. Eighty per cent of the population were Negro and the authorities rigged the election, claiming that the ballot boxes had been lost. One of the main aims of the SNCC go-to-the-people offensive was to encourage the Negroes to go to the polls, while the Whites' counter-offensive was to create a paralysis of fear and let the Black masses know they have nothing to lose but their nightmares.

The country is racist, they said repeatedly, and it doesn't take much to prove. The White man has been given 'one more chance' once too often. The Black man no longer believes in one more chance for the Whites, because it means less and less chance for the Blacks. They believe there is a patent connection between the situation of the White world outside and the racial happenings within America. To counter this effectively, Blacks of the world, 500 million strong, should separate into one unit, build their own economy and civilisation. Whether they re-combine eventually with the White bloc would then depend on whether the Whites develop from their present level of cut-throat animality to the level of civilised human beings.

To date, Integration—physically, politically, and culturally—has meant the attempt of Blacks to move into White neighbourhoods, paying for their thwarted efforts with their own blood. This is no coming together of equals, which is what Integration should be. Till the economic basis for genuine equality amongst all peoples is laid, all talk of Integration is a fraud. The tragedy of the Black man is that he has been a victim of this fraud too patiently, too peacefully, too long.

So that I should see for myself, they decided to walk me through the slums of the ghetto to the SNCC business office at 142 Vine Street. It is hardly credible that a place with a name as romantic as Vine City should turn out to be the very entrails of Hell. The streets were broken, sparsely tarred, and pock-marked with ditches. Old shacks squatted alongside the streets like curious squashed match boxes put together by some pack rat builder with a sick sense of humour. Here and there these 'houses' were patched with rust-eaten car bonnets in place of glass windows—the cold had to be kept out somehow.

I saw Black men and Black women, citizens of the American affluent society, crouching on doorsteps like little animals, chained to their pillars of poverty by ever-thickening cords of discriminating Yankee capitalism. Some of them strolled about aimlessly as if it were a public holiday. Jobs weren't scarce; they were nonexistent. Young women, who under different circumstances would have been paragons of beauty, sauntered along the streets, battered and worn by the degradation of the one ready job, prostitution. Beneath their eyes, lines of suffering plastered over with cheap talcum powder were nevertheless visible, like little worms smothered to death with a paste of araba ash. You could easily tell from the 'high' look in their eyes that they had indeed learned to smoke.

On one corner of the street, hemmed in by shacks, was a little rough clearing which was supposed to be a children's playground. Even that, I was told, had been a recent innovation generously introduced to improve the lot of the kids. And as I watched those pathetic half-naked children running on rough gravel without shoes, I wondered if they knew what the future held in store for them. Indeed, the slums of Vine City, like the slums of Harlem I was to discover later, were a lamentable testimony to man's inhumanity to man—and this was in a country which professes to go to the faraway Vietnams of this world to prevent Vietnamese inhumanity to other Vietnamese.

At one point, as we came to a rise at the end of the street, I looked into a distant White area and saw a new Pentagonlike skyscraper shooting up into the heavens as if to mock the poverty-stricken ghetto dwellers of Vine City.

'What building is that?' I asked one of the boys. 'What will they do with it when it's finished?'

'I don't know, brother,' one boy replied with unnerving quietness. 'But I can tell you one thing for sure. That goddam house ain't gonna stand there for long. I have a feeling somebody's gonna mow it down with dynamite real soon.'

'Yeah,' the rest joined in, and began to chant in growing frenzy, 'Burn, baby, burn!'

I was relieved when the night finally came and they took me to the hostel where they all lived like dauntless crusaders. After I had changed into my African national robes, they treated me to the most moving reception party of my American tour. Forgetting all the trials and tribulations of mankind for a few hours, we wined and dined and guffawed and sang revolutionary songs about Lumumba, Nkrumah, Odinga and Black Mother Africa. This was all the more significant to me because I had been warned before I left London that the Negro in America totally dissociates himself from Africa and looks down upon everything and everyone 'African'. In my experience, however, for the average Afro-American family to have an 'African' visitor home for dinner was something akin to a status symbol. Not only did they implore me to come to dinner in my national costume and give the invariably packed party a 'back to Africa' touch, they even insisted on my coming to breakfast if all my dinner times were already booked for the period of my stay.

It was in the early hours of the morning that I returned to the Peach Tree Hotel. As I lay down on my bed, pondering my experiences of the past hours, it was all too clear to me that the fun had ended with the last echo of laughter and that, with the approaching dawn, I would once again be wading through the realities of the worst Hell on this earth, the Hell of the American deep south. And even that is only a slice of the truth. For the whole of America is the Black man's Hell.

And even that is not the whole truth. For America is also

the Red man's Hell.

My visit to the Indian Reservation in New Mexico stirred the innermost fibres of my being. The fact that the original settler of what is now America has been squeezed into a position where he has hardly a place to lay his blanket is an impression which will remain indelibly in my mind as long as I live.

I can still hear the quiet voice of the Jemez Indian Chief counselling me with all the reserved dignity of a king. 'Never let anyone take away your culture from you, son. Because once it's gone, you'll never get it back.'

He was a little old sage with intelligent, laughing eyes, and he received me in the sitting-room of his red adobe bungalow. Though he was small in stature, his presence was overwhelming. His clothes consisted simply of an ordinary cotton shirt, tight long pants and a red band around his head. This was how he remained except once when we posed for a photograph. He rose, threw a folded red blanket over his shoulder, placed a regal, embroidered leather medallion around his neck, and held his royal sceptre in his hand.

Otherwise, reserved and withdrawn, he sat quietly till he had listened to my explanation of the purpose of my visit. After scrutinising me carefully and weighing my every word, he was disposed to talk and chatted most amiably without losing his fatherly deportment. Those who think that Yogi Maharishi Maheshiogi is the sage of the age should go to New Mexico and meet Paramount Chief Picos of the Jemez Indian Pueblo.

Making me sit on the sofa beside him, he answered all my questions with quiet dignity, telling me all about the internal administration of his pueblo, the history and philosophical attitudes of his people, the cultural and religious ties between the people of his pueblo and seventeen other pueblos in New Mexico, the attitudes of his people towards America and the 'modern' world generally, and his personal dreams and visions of the future. I marvelled at this man's knowledge—and who will blame me after I had seen for years the Hollywood portrayal of American Indians. I found plenty to love in the Indian way of life, and certainly a great deal to learn from it.

I was there when a burly-looking Indian youth came in and, seeing from the chief's countenance that his presence was unwelcome, thrust something into the old man's hand, bowed respectfully, and walked out again. When the young man had gone, the chief unclenched his hand, displaying a thick wad of dollar bills. Apparently the young man had smuggled a bottle of liquor from his place of work in the city into the pueblo and been caught in this unforgivable infringement of the pueblo law. The elders, under the chairmanship of the chief, had sat in judgement over this man, found him guilty, and levied a fine of thirty-five dollars on him. That was what he had come in to pay.

'I never allow alcohol in this compound,' stated the old man with grim finality. 'And as long as I am the governor here, I will never allow any White man's bad habits to infiltrate my compound and deprave my people.'

I left the Jemez Pueblo with plenty to chew over in my mind. I went away resolved never again to listen to anyone selling me the idea that the American Indian is a self-immolating xenophobe whose life is founded on war dances and an inherent aversion from self-improvement. I carried away the horrifying picture of what Africa could easily become if pig-headed politicians and Sandhurst-trained gunmen continue to sell us out to those traditional bearers of the White man's burden whose God-given duty is to castrate non-White natives all over the world.

I met White Americans who, with not uncharacteristic flippancy, explained away the Indian Reservations as the White man's painful duty to respect the Red man's wish for undisturbed isolation. But they never told me that this isolation, supposedly so respected, so sacrosanct, so undisturbed by the Whites, is negated when they draft the Red man into the White man's army to fight the White man's battles.

We hear about the Red man's aversion from modernisation, when the truth is that no people on this earth will reject modernisation and industrialisation unless that 'modernisation' seeks to destroy the culture which it professes to strengthen. People are reluctant to accept 'modernisation'

which in fact threatens to subject their culture to another
culture which they consider alien and inferior to their own.
Like every visitor on a cultural tour of the United States,
I never ceased to hear about the Red man's reluctance to
change. I saw the evidence of this 'reluctance' while I was
there. Yes, I saw it in Indian-owned cars, bicycles and
modern lorries driven all over the pueblo; I saw it in
Governor Picos's colour television set and the forest of television aerials growing over the pueblo roof-tops; I saw it
in the Indian's willingness to send his children to city schools
in Alburquerque—and saw the White man's unwillingness
to open wide the gates of knowledge to these 'reluctant'
people. Instead, Indian children are herded, apartheid
fashion, into a separate school of their own for fear their
inherent inferiority might rub off on White children and
lower White standards.

'The native does not want to mix!' White Americans say
with eagerness. It is not without a familiar ring. You hear
it in Australia. You hear it in Canada. You hear it in South
Africa. You hear it loudest today in Zimbabwe. You hear
it in any part of this world where a handful of greedy Whites
are prepared to destroy human values by lying, cheating, distorting history and profaning defenceless men in order to
lay their hands on the property of their victim.

'I have no spur to prick the sides of my intent,' moaned
Shakespeare through the lips of Macbeth, 'but only vaulting
ambition, which o'erleaps itself and falls on the other.'
Shakespeare knew his people well.

To contemplate the sufferings of the American Indian is
disturbing enough. To go there and actually see these
sufferings against a background of the magic, the splendour
and the beauty of the surrounding Indian country is simply
unbearable, like watching a wingless new-hatched fledgeling
preyed upon by white ants.

I stood there and watched this magnificent expanse of
Indian country till tear drops stood in my eyes. I have seen
beautiful spectacles in my life countless times; I have stood
amidst the white hills of tropical Iyiegbuoma back home
and watched the sun set the way nobody else knows it in

the world except the select villagers of Eziora; I have kept vigil on the banks of the great Niger and watched the tides come and the surfs doing the silk dance; I have stayed awake at night drinking 'illicit' gin and watching the stars dancing over the blue lakes of Olu Jungle while wild cats howled away in the distance and half-naked brown women breast-fed their cooing babies in the moonlight; I have travelled to Senegal and made love to the most beautiful woman in Dakar while her husband was outside the door, sharpening a hatchet rather noisily on a grinding stone and asking the servants within my hearing distance how thick my neck was; I have trekked all the way up and all the way down the majestic spirals of the legendary Milken Hill of Enugu Coal City while the cocks crowed in the dead hours of the morning; I have even retired like a hermit to the cave zones of Holywell Bay to drink in the beauty of nature in the serenity and wizardry of Cornwall's undiscovered far country; but never before in my life have I been so cowed, as I was that day, by the bewitching majesty and magic of the New Mexican Indian country.

Towering up with pyramidal elegance were countless mountains; white hills, black hills, red hills, indigo hills— all colours of the rainbow—jutted out like the fantastic Mountains of the Moon in a splendour far beyond the powers of poetry to describe. To see all this fluorescing between a setting sun and a rising full moon was enchantment itself. No wonder, I gasped, the Indians fought so hard to keep this earthly paradise to themselves. The sky was a miracle of cloud-formations, the landscape so vast and peaceful that there was no need even for the trees to grow too close together—and didn't they know it!

Miles and miles of beautiful country stretched to the horizon. Everything here seemed larger than life. One soon begins to understand the simplicity and humility of the Indian life and religion. For who can gaze at Stupendousness itself, for centuries dominating this vast landscape, without being quailed into the acceptance that man is but a tiny insect crawling about on a little pond-holding rock called Earth.

From Albuquerque to Santa Fé I roamed, and from Santa Fé to Los Alamos, climbing mountains at dawn and dipping into moon-drenched sulphur springs at night. It has been said that the first White man went to New Mexico in search of the fabled Seven Cities of Gold. Later generations followed in search of silver, oil and uranium. Some have gone purely in search of solace, rare in the cut-throat jungle of the North. I, probably the first African tramp to arrive, had gone there simply in search of the truth. And, in spite of the bitterness of the truth I found, I went away resolved that if ever I decide to retire and die in some serene isolation outside my native town of Ozubulu, it will be to New Mexico that I must surely return.

Flying out of New Mexico and into California was a different story. It meant the end of a perfect honeymoon with spiritual bliss, and the beginning of another voyage within the racial chamber of horrors America calls The States. Los Angeles is a special case. Everything she does, she does with a vengeance. She evokes the greatest glamour and produces the worst scum; she makes top millionaires overnight, and topples twice as many into bankruptcy in half the time; her dream is Hollywood, her reality is Watts. Here the Whites hate the idea of integration almost as keenly as they love the practice in bed; and the Negroes, who began by hankering after both the idea and the practice, have ended up being betrayed by both.

I was in a barber's shop in Watts one day; the barber thrust a little booklet into my hand. As I turned through the pages, my eyes caught a poem by Jack Markham called 'Imminent Hate'. I remember this poem particularly, not just out of professional interest, but because it reflects both the mood of the Negro in the ghetto and the Negro's attitude toward religion and God at this time. I reproduce this poem here because nothing I write as an outsider could reproduce the mood with more clarity and feeling than this Afro-American has. He was obviously verbalising the innermost convictions of his heart, a heart which, whether one approves of it or not, is the heart of the new Black America—a vital force in the history of the new Third World, the force that

must decide the future course of mankind by forcing the
White world of power into imminent confrontation with
itself.

> You'll make us hate you yet, I fear,
> You dominators of the Earth,
> For you say you're right when you know you err,
> And you robbed us gradually, from birth.
> Although the facts of your history
> Are recorded by you with pride,
> My God, Religion, and Nationality
> Emerge as vague bromides.

> You told us God was in the sky,
> And the ultimate was heaven's street,
> But do you seek the Sweet Bye and Bye?
> No! You're ever robbing me at my feet!
> And too, the women depicted up there;
> The angels so blonde and white,
> Why, I'm afraid to succumb to Pearl Gate,
> You might lynch me on sight!

> Religion might be a virtue inducer,
> And man's guide to the stars,
> But if I meet you—(Excuse me Lord),
> I'll detour on to Mars!
> 'Love one another' in spite, you said,
> Turn cheek, both right and left,
> If soon I don't rest my paining slapped head,
> I'll be tempted to kill myself.

> The physical slavery that we did see,
> Under you for three hundred years,
> Gave you time to distort our history,
> Oh! The rattle of chains in my ears!
> You kept us away from schools and books,
> And raped our women as you pleased,
> And lynched us by reason of only 'one look',
> Your derelictions have never ceased!

Oh, that joyous day when the slaves were freed,
Their eyes were aglow,
Too trusting to know they had been deceived,
They still wore the stigma 'Negro'.
How long do you think I'll be pacified,
With a vision of heaven's street,
A job yet to find, a pint of wine,
And a History that doesn't speak?

This was the language and mood I was to encounter from now on as I tramped the Black ghettos of America and delved into the soul of the grass roots. It was the mood of Watts in Los Angeles; it was the mood of the Philmoore District in San Francisco; it was the mood of the Black Bottom in Detroit; it was the mood of Central Avenue in Cleveland; it was the mood of Sower Street in Philadelphia; it was the mood of 47th Street in Southside Chicago; it was the mood I met, ate, drank, slept and chimed blues to in 125th Street, Harlem; it was indeed the Negro mood. In fact, in a book actually called *The Negro Mood*, this was how my friend, Lerone Bennett, summarised it:

Less than one hundred years ago, Nietzsche announced to a startled world that God was dead. Religion apart, he was announcing a psychological fact, the death of God in the heart of his contemporaries. What we have to deal with today is a psychological fact of a similar dimension. The white man is dead. He died at Auschwitz and Buchenwald. He died at Hiroshima. He died in Montgomery and Birmingham and Little Rock. The white man is dead. Men with pale skin still live. But the idea of a man with a certain color skin and a mandate from God to order and regulate the lives of men with darker skins; that idea is dead—in Panama and in Kenya, in Milwaukee and in Mississippi. We no longer live in a world controlled by that idea, though some people, Negroes and Whites, have not read the obituary notices.

But the one man who had read this obituary notice long before Lerone Bennett was a man known to the world as

Elijah Muhammad, Messenger of Allah, leader and founder of the American (Black) Muslims. My meeting with him in his home in Chicago was without doubt the highlight of my American tour.

The incidents which led to that meeting were in themselves remarkable. The previous day I had attended the Muslim Service at the Temple of Islam No. 2 in Southside Chicago. I arrived a little late and was stupefied to see that everyone present was immaculately groomed in a dinner suit and black bow tie. And the Muslim Guards, in their blue uniforms and star-studded round hats, looked like a regiment from a superior planet. They were tall, handsome, and very disciplined. In my casual dress—simple sports jacket and grey, tight slacks, I looked like a real Teddy boy in their midst.

With their unfailing polite smiles, the guards told me nicely but firmly that no one, not even an invited guest like myself, was allowed into the temple not properly dressed in a dark suit. This was in accord with Messenger Elijah's aim of making the Black man respectable. To expect respect from others, you must communicate respectability. Elijah's law, they said, could not afford to be a respecter of persons. I saw their point, especially as they offered to provide me with a car and driver to take me all the way back to Manor House Hotel, wait for me to change into proper attire, and bring me back again to the Temple in time for the service.

More curious than ever, I accepted the offer and, in less than half an hour, was back. They escorted me straight to a reception room in the Islam University block adjoining the mosque. Here I was welcomed by one of the 'Brothers' with the same customary disarming politeness and smile. He gave me a form to fill in but, for some reason, insisted that he write the particulars down himself while I dictated the necessary information. It was soon plain that literacy was not his forte. Apart from the difficulty of printing the letters one after the other laboriously till a word was completed, when he got to the dotted space for my profession, he printed in bold letters 'RITER'. I had nothing but respect for this lean, aging man when I found out that, until a month before

when he had been released from jail, he had been totally
illiterate. Not only had the Muslims cured him of drug
addiction, thuggery and slow self-destruction, they had in
one month's time instilled into him enough self-awareness
and pride for him to transform and dedicate himself to a
life of spiritual guidance to others less fortunate in order
that they, too, could follow the same road to self-education
and nobility of spirit he himself had trod.

The Muslim 'Sisters' milled around like a band of angels,
clad in immaculate white robes and long head tunics. Their
faces, dusky and beautiful like a bevy of Nefertitis, glowed
through the white wraps like the sombre lustre of the setting
sun. Spiritual contentment and love shone in their eyes as
they welcomed new members into their fold. That disarming Muslim smile, the first thing one notices about these
Muslims, looked even more infectious when radiated by the
girls. At first, I wondered whether they were pulling my leg.
But I soon became engulfed by the sheer force of their
genuineness. There was something about the presence of
these Black Muslims, even when I was in the company of
the most formidable man alive, Muhammad Ali, which made
me feel that, for the first time in my life, I was meeting real
human beings. With the Muslim Sisters, this quality seemed
even more pronounced. They wore no make-up, displayed
no phoney airs, no artificialities. You can therefore imagine
the awe of everyone present when a youth, looking at one of
the 'Sisters', suddenly declared:

'Isn't she a witch!'

'Man,' cried his friend, horrified, 'you are crazy. What did
you say a thing like that for?'

'Baby,' came the reply, 'only a witch can go about producing this paralysing effect on people just by parting a pair
of lips in a smile.'

The role of the Negro woman in the Black revolution is
something which has fascinated me for some time, even long
before I went to the States. From the outset, the Negro
woman in America has always enjoyed a privileged position
compared to her male. The Whites have always preferred
to integrate with her when confronted with a choice, and

have given her a job, even if only mopping the floor, while her husband stayed at home, with wounded pride. In this way, the Negro housewife has come to be the accepted bread-winner and consequently the esteemed boss in the household while the husband's authority has been virtually whittled down to nil. Potentially, therefore, the sexes have been re-versed in the Negro household and, on a communal level, the Negro women have come to constitute a new class of white-collar workers.

With the emergence of the new Negro revolution, there-fore, the Negro woman is in a dilemma. Must she now join hands with the Negro male and fight the very White man who, after all, has given her the privileged position she enjoys, or is it wiser to ignore the noise of battle and, with the indirect support of silence, help the Whites sustain the status quo in which she has a vested interest? Must she join the Negro revolution and help bring about the liberation of Blacks, male and female, or is it more sensible to use her privileged position to be the vanguard of a world-wide struggle for female emancipation, Black and White? Is she woman first and Negro second, or Negro first and woman second?

I must say I was moved by the sheer energy and devotion of the Muslim girls, who had obviously made their choice. They had chosen to stand by the fathers of their children and champion the cause of revolution which, with proper ideological orientation, must surely be the beginning of the end for those who want to keep the dispossessed permanently dispossessed, male and female.

At the mosque entrance, I was handed over to a band of Muslim guards for another routine preliminary prior to going into the Temple. I was searched from head to toe. Still wearing their customary smiles and making small talk (Have you been long in Chicago, sir? . . . Do you like it? . . .) they left no pocket unturned, no article unexamined, no part of me unsearched for concealed weapons. That was how, I was told afterwards, they came to discover on one occasion that a male visitor had three balls between his thighs, one of which turned out to be a hand grenade. Yes, it was a thorough search, to say the least.

The search over, they apologised most profusely for subjecting me to this treatment and hoped I would appreciate why no one could be rated above suspicion—their enemies were mighty and plentiful and would stop at nothing to blast them out of existence—Allah knew they had tried and would try again IN VAIN.

At long last, the gates of the Temple yawned before me, and with the voice of Minister James 3X thundering from the pulpit in front, I stepped inside . . .

The next morning, I was woken up by a rather early telephone call, at 6.30 am.

'My name is John Ali,' a voice said at the other end. 'I am the General Secretary of the Muslims. We met yesterday after the service, with Muhammad Ali.'

'Yes, I remember you well,' I replied.

'How would you feel about meeting the Messenger of Allah himself, Mr Elijah Muhammad?'

'I would love that very much,' I replied.

'Mr Muhammad has said the pleasure will be his.' Note the choice of words. 'He requests you to be his guest of honour at dinner in his home tonight.'

'Splendid. Tonight suits me fine.'

'I'll pick you up at 5.25 p.m. at the Temple.'

I was a quarter of an hour late but John Ali was patient and smiling, as if being kept waiting was a treat for him. We went into the Islam University block from the front and, going right through, emerged into a side street where a car was waiting. From there we raced to Mr Muhammad's Hyde Park home. John unlocked the front door with a special key of his own and led me straight to the bathroom to wash my hands according to Muslim custom.

As I stepped out of the room, I felt a hand touch me on the shoulder. I started and turned.

'My name is Elijah Muhammad,' said a little man standing before me. He took my hand in his, shook it with fatherly affection, grinning disarmingly. At first, I couldn't believe my eyes. Was it possible, I pondered, that this diminutive person was the Elijah Muhammad, the leader and teacher of

America since the death of El-Hajj Malik El-Shabazz, the most powerful Black man since Marcus Garvey and certainly the most mysterious religious leader in the world? He did not look quite as frail as I had been led to believe, but he did cough a bit. Dressed as if to fit his publicity photo, he was indeed a 'man in his mid-sixties, 5 feet 6 inches high, scaling the modest weight of 150 pounds.' Negro-brown and bald, he wore his famed dark suit and bow tie. It seemed so silly to introduce myself in return, even if formally, for I had the uncanny feeling that he knew every move I had made from the moment I set foot in Chicago.

In an atmosphere of profound quiet, he led me into an inner dining-room where members of his household were waiting, all seated at table in sepulchral silence, waiting for our entrance. It was most dramatic. I must confess that I found this the most unnerving moment of my American experience, but once the Messenger began to talk, he had a way of drawing me so completely into his power and presence that, converted or not, I was soon to become conscious of nothing else in the world except a universe strained between Allah and 'the blue-eyed devil'.

Then came the introduction of his household. At one table in the corner sat his secretaries, looking very beautiful in their ankle-reaching dresses. There were usually four of them, he explained, but one was indisposed and in bed. It was to this team of four secretaries that he dictated his daily letters, speeches, newspaper articles and special messages, from the breakfast table at 7.30 in the morning till late at night. On our own table, Mr Muhammad himself naturally was at the head, having beckoned me to sit at the other end, facing him. On his immediate right was his wife; and next to her, nearest to me, was the Principal of the University of Islam, the lady who had replaced Sister Christine X, the author of *Muhammad's Children*. (Sister Christine left the Muslims with Malcolm X during the Great Split.) On the Messenger's immediate left was John Ali, and next to him was another Muslim 'Brother' who kept nudging and urging me in whispers all through the dinner to fire every question I had at the old man because this was my 'great chance to get the truth from the horse's mouth.' I did. But my conversation with Elijah, the study and analysis of the Muslim philosophy and Elijah's place in the history of Black Revolution is a subject which deserves a book of its own.

I was deeply concerned at this time with a new revolutionary force which was sweeping America like a tropical fire. It was a force I could understand very well, for that same fire had been burning in my own soul long before I discovered it was common to Black youth of my generation all over the world. Frustration is compelling us all, wherever we are born, to rethink our position.

All men are born free. It is men who make slaves of other men. It is therefore absurd, as the generations before us have done, to talk about making people free. You can only talk about stopping oppression. There is no such thing as the abolition of Slavery. You can only talk about destruction of Masterhood. There is no such thing as the Negro problem. What we should be talking about is the White problem. We should be talking about the nuisance-value of a race of people who, because of an illusion about the colour of their skin, are determined by words and deeds to subject the rest of mankind to economic, cultural and political dependency and slavery. And talking about it is not enough either. Because, according to an old Chinese proverb, 'the wind of words alone cannot turn the mill of history.'

For too many years, Black people in different parts of the world have been suffering at the hands of Whites what they believe to be isolated pockets of oppression. Hence the Black peoples of Britain think that the Black man's problem will be over once Brixton, Paddington and Perry Bar are 'integrated'. Hence the African in Nigeria once thought that 'Independence' for his country meant that the Black man could live in freedom. Hence the Indian worker in Bombay once believed that the problem of the Black man in the Caribbean was different from his own. Hence millions of Africans in Southern Africa sincerely believe that it is only a handful of White settlers who are keeping them down and actually expect the White men of Britain to come to their aid. Hence the Afro-American of Detroit thought, until recently, that his White oppressor was a different man from the White oppressor of the Vietnamese people . . .

Today we know differently, of course. We know that, in spite of the threadbare old strategy of divide-and-conquer practised by Whites, Black peoples all over the world, wherever they are born, wherever they go, drink the same waters of affliction from the hands of the same man: the White man. We know that the Negro of Harlem in New York has much more in common with the African in Angola than he has with his White neighbour in Manhattan. We know that the attitude of White people to the Blacks all over the world is the same. We know that in America, Black people are being lynched by Anglo-Saxon fascists; and that in Canada, Anglo-Saxon fascism has crystallised into European Preferential Migration and the Anti-Asiatic Act. We know that in Australia, Anglo-Saxon civilisation has typically enshrined itself as the White Australia Policy; and that in South Africa, it has escalated to the dizzy heights of Apartheid. We know that in Rhodesia, Anglo-Saxon fascism is rearing its head as UDI, and that the White world, in spite of the lip-deep pious protestations of kith-and-kin statesmen, is applauding the 'rebel' Smith regime.

While we see that when we pinpoint the areas of the world's most brutal and despicable racisms today, they coincide with the Anglo-Saxon dispersion, we also know that, on an individual level, the only difference between the Ian Smiths and Harold Wilsons of the White world is not a difference in principle, but a difference in tactics. We know they are both agreed that the African is an inferior being incapable of administrating his own community. The only difference is that while the Smiths say this is a permanent impairment, the Wilsons, for pragmatic reasons, say that in time the White man's kiss-of-life might possibly wake up the African and start him developing from his present state of being three-quarters human to a state where he becomes a European who just looks like an African. We know that the quarrel between the Smiths and Wilsons is not a quarrel between fascism and anti-fascism, but a quarrel between frankness and hypocrisy within a fascist framework.

In a word, the Black peoples of the world have found out that what they are facing today is not, as they were once told, isolated pockets of White oppression, but International White Power. And that, isolated, the Black men are weak and unable to fight from their minority position. But united, they are strong and very much in the majority.

Yet majority without action is impotent. This Black impotency has been exploited by the enemies of the Black people too often, too long, too ruthlessly. What Black people need, as a guide for action, is a revolutionary philosophy which will educate them to be not only reactive, but also active—a philosophy which must teach the Black man, especially the Uncle Tom who giggles when it doesn't tickle and scratches where it doesn't itch, that man, as Frantz Fanon pointed out, is not only YES . . .yes to life, yes to love, yes to generosity; but also that man is equally NO . . .no to scorn, no to degradation, no to exploitation, no to the butchery of what is most human in man: freedom. This philosophy the new Negro of America has begun to call Black Power.

Black Power. I found from experience that, to appreciate the true definition of Black Power, one must first negate the negative definitions of the sensational press. Black Power is not 'indefinable'. It is not a slogan of dissident Blacks. It is not Black fascism. It does not mean the demand of every White head on a platter. It does not even mean Black domination of the world. To understand the true meaning of the concept of Black Power and how it came about at a certain stage in the psychological dialectic of the American Negro, it is best to take the two words, *Black* and *Power* separately.

Black. For centuries, the Black man in America has chased after a mirage. This mirage he has called *integration.* It is a mirage because America is traditionally a segregated society. De facto America consists of Irish quarters, Jewish quarters, German quarters, and as many other quarters as Europe has tribes. There are China Towns of San Francisco and New York. There is the Amish Intercourse of Pennsylvania. The ghettos where the Negroes are packed in animalistic isolation are well known. Puerto Ricans inevitably live in segregated communities. Even the country's oldest settler, the American Indian, is not yet integrated into White society. It is therefore unrealistic for the Negro to seek integration in a society so obviously segregated by tradition.

But there was a reason why the Negro not only sought this 'integration' but was, in fact, the only racial group that wanted it so intensely. One of the saddest consequences of Negro history is that, while every other racial group in America enjoys a cultural linkage with her past, the Negro was brutally and suddenly cut off from his own. And, not unnaturally, the Negro was obliged to turn to the society of his White master for cultural sustenance and 'integration'. But the door of White society was slammed in his face. He was segregated. He was lynched. He was frozen out and thrown into the ghetto to stifle in cultural frustration.

Contrary to White expectation, this became for the Negro a blessing in disguise. The cultural rebuff of the Whites galvanised him into a desperate quest for his past. And the emergence of New African nations, in his land of origin, brought to the open very telling historical facts about his past. Africa was never a cultural vacuum as alleged by Whites. The Negro realises he has been the victim of a lie and that White cultural superiority is only a White-fabricated tale to dupe the Black man and to provide an excuse for dehumanising the rest of mankind. He sees that 'White = Beautiful' and 'Black = Ugly and Evil' are untrue equations, morally, culturally, historically; and that their purpose has only been to convert materials connected with White values and culture into commodities which are exchangeable with the raw materials of those other lands which the White man covets.

Suddenly, the Negro is no longer the Black American ashamed of any identification with his African past; he becomes a hyphenated American, the Afro-American. This has signalled the birth of Negro cultural nationalism in America and, with it, the Negro's rediscovery of Africa. The Negro woman no longer burns her hair to 'Whiten' it, aping White values as those Japanese women do who operate on their eyes to cut them into round 'White' shapes. Instead of the I-used-to-be-a-Negro straight hairdos, the Black woman is now beginning to wear the 'Natural Hair Style' with pride. Afro-American schools of culture have sprung up everywhere like mushrooms and the Negro has been teaching himself Swahili and other African languages with ardour. In New York and Washington, DC, l'Africana djellabah has become the vogue. In San Francisco, Sara Fabio has written fiery poetry about the Burning Spears of Africa. In Atlanta, Georgia, as well as in Watts, culture-voracious SNCC youths have been chanting 'Odinga Odinga' with love.

In Chicago, Phillip Cohran, having electrified African musical instruments and given weekly performances at the Harper Theatre, staggered the White world when he declared that White classical music was 'unnatural' and profane, and he proceeded to invent his Originalist musical philosophy to prove his case.

All over America, Toms with the House-Nigger mentality have fast reached the autumn of their days and the tide of Black cultural nationalism has been sweeping a new generation of Carmichaels to the fore. From now onwards, *Black* in Black Power has come to mean for this new generation of Afro-Americans that 'our nose is broad, our lips thick, our skin black, and *we are beautiful.*'

Power. Black cultural nationalism without economic power is a sham. And under the present world system where the line of Colour has coincided with the line of Class, no Black man in his right mind can be expected to carry innocence to the point of believing he can seek and get this power within the existing White camp. To seek economic power within this White social structure could only mean a replacement of exploitation of Black by White with exploitation of Black by Black, a mere displacement of colour discrimination by class discrimination.

Since the objective is the annihilation of oppression, not the butchery of colour, this would be unsuitable. The only way the Black man can get real *power* is by smashing the system that incubates exploitation of the Blacks. If he cannot smash this system from within, he must set in motion an international revolutionary force which will do so from without. The Black man must either smash that system or the system will take advantage of his docility and smash him. From the foregoing analysis of the two words, *Black* and *Power*, one can summarily define Black Power as the totality of the economic, cultural, political and, if necessary, military power which the Black people of the world need to abolish White oppression.

The America that I saw represents the epitome of this White oppression.

It will perhaps surprise some people that, after touring the length and breadth of the United States during what must have been the 'hottest' summer in American experience, after wading through the riotous cauldron of the North and penetrating the Klan-ridden hell of the South, after meeting the men and women who allegedly make America tick and the teeming masses who, like me, have become victims of that ticking, after conferring with Congressmen and Senators in Washington, DC (Big Deal!) and then being a guest-of-honour to the Messenger of Allah himself in South-side Chicago, after seeing the beauty and beauties of New Mexico and the ugliest ugliness of the inside of the Indian Reservation, it will perhaps surprise some people that, after all these moving experiences, I have here pushed masses and masses of these 'worthier' materials to the periphery to make a central issue of Dolores, a little black prostitute from Harlem.

I hope this does not surprise you too, my dear beautiful sister, Dolores. For this sort of thing only surprises those people to whom the dignity of man means nothing, and the dignity of woman even less. Even if all this long talk in this long letter means nothing else to you, I want you to understand that I care. If you can fully understand and accept that, I promise you that, even behind bars in this heart of Babylon, I will feel good inside my heart.

I care. I did what I did because I care. I care deeply, I care. I stopped myself from having you cheaply because I care. I refused to denigrate you, Black mother, even if it

meant throwing you out of my hotel room for that same
reason. I care. Oh my God, I care. I care because I love you.
I love you because you are my sister. You are my sister
because—what else could you be but my sister?

All sorts of things went through my head in that hotel
room. In that fraction of a second, the tragic history that is
yours and mine reeled through my head like a silent film. I
asked myself all sorts of questions concerning you, me, and
Man. And every time, I came back to the same nagging
paramount question. How could I prove that you were not
really my sister!

In my little village in Africa, we have a great tradition of
the extended family. I asked myself whether this Black girl
I was about to dive into was not really my blood sister? How
could I be sure that I was not about to graft my penis into
the black xylem of my family tree?

There was only one way I could have told that. And that
was by the language you spoke. But you no longer speak a
Black tongue today because of the cruel and brutal consequences of slave history.

In those days, it was against the slave law for Black slaves
to speak their native tongues. Those who defied this law
were known to have been shot on the spot or, if still in
transit, thrown into the sea alive to be devoured by sharks.
That was how you, my dear Black sister, were stripped of
your language, your culture, your dignity, your pride and
inevitably your human rights. You are the end product of
a macabre history which saw the kidnapping and forced
transportation of fifty million Black men and women from
Africa to the Western slave-plantation within two hundred
years. Yours was the background of a history in which
legitimate reign of terror was the only way of converting
human beings into beasts of burden by professional 'slave
breakers'. Those who were wounded had ashes, salt and
cinders poured into their wounds. Many were castrated and
mutilated, some had their ears notched or chopped off, others
were burned, roasted alive or simply packed with gun-
powder and blown up. The not so lucky were oiled and
salted and then fed alive to insects. So satanic did this sort

of practice become that the twenty per cent of the slave
population who died annually on passage were considered,
when all was said and done, the luckiest of the slaves.

Women slaves got the worst of the brunt. They were raped,
brutalised, and dehumanised in unspeakable ways. They
were not even spared the ordeal of lynching. Cases were
numerous where unborn babies slid off the wombs of pregnant women dangling on lynch trees. And as these babies
fell to the ground, the rabid lynch mobs rushed forward
with sadistic glee to dance over and trample the little infant
to a pulpy death. This was excusable because it was considered cheaper to buy a new slave from Africa than to waste
the White master's money and time rearing up a baby slave
from infancy to manhood.

These incidents were neither rare nor isolated but indeed
a fundamental and integral part of the slave hustle. So
frequent did they become, so profitable did the slave master
find this cruel hustling of Black flesh, and so despicable did
the slave find his condition that instances were many when
slaves committed suicide, not to escape suffering, but just
to spite their masters. Such, my dear Black sister, is the
heritage of Black living death you have borne through no
fault of yours. You are a genuine article of the Black Harlem
I saw, typical of many Black men and women who, though
delivered still-born into a cruel environment, still go on
walking. They have done this to you.

Yet this is not the end of the story. For, right now in my
mind's eye, I can still see you as you were that night in that
hotel room. Stripped to the last pubic fibre of your dignity,
you were grovelling on your knees like a little slave woman,
taking off the shoes of your purchaser, and getting all set to
engulf his urinary pipe in your mouth, re-enacting that
macabre history all over again.

But there was a difference this time though. And it wasn't
slight. The ruthless slave purchaser was no longer the White
man. Certainly not that night in the hotel room. The Black
man had taken over where the White man left off. This was
the role in which I saw myself that night. In one fleeting
fraction of a second, I had looked into the long mirror by

the bed-side and seen myself standing there, undoing my buttons like a lusty slave-breaker, while you, like a choiceless Black slave-woman of old, were on your knees, getting ready to zip down my pants and bury your head between my lap, like a helpless little lamb sucking its mother. I felt so sick with myself that I couldn't stand the scene a moment longer. I never felt so uptight in my life. That was why I leapt back so suddenly and ordered you to quit it and split.

I was not angry with you. I was angry with myself. Contrary to what you thought, it was not the nakedness of your body that sickened me. At that precise moment, it was the nakedness of my soul. I repeat without hesitation what I said at the beginning of this letter. You are the most beautiful woman I have ever seen in the nude. I would like to say a lot more but I can't. They censor our letters here. The worst thing about prison is not being allowed to make decisions. But don't grieve for me. I have long come to the conclusion that the Black man has no right to live like a man till he learns to die like a man. Bernard Shaw once wrote that history is full of examples of men and women who have embraced death to avoid destruction.

I remember an article I read a few weeks ago. It told a sad little story about a Vietcong girl who had been killed in battle. A love letter found on her body revealed how lonely she had been for a man she knew she might never see again. She had loved him deeply and yet left him behind to go into the jungle to die for her convictions. Her letter contained the saddest line a woman ever wrote to her man: 'When my little lamp goes out, I hold your shadow in my arms.'

You couldn't wish anyone a nobler death, male or female. I can now hear the rattling of keys and footsteps on the landing. That means the warders are coming to switch off the lights for the night. I cannot promise to hold your shadow in my arms, having failed you once as a lover, but I do promise that from now till my dying day, I will never cease thinking of you as a sister among sisters. Goodnight.

Your brother,

Obi.

A Word About My Home

(Written towards the end of the 'Biafran' War)

THE BODY of a seven-year-old boy lay at the foot of an anthill, cold and stiff. It was lying in a pool of his caking blood and the vultures were already hovering overhead. His skull had been smashed in by a bullet and the rest of him was also riddled with bullets. Even if he had lived, he would not have been able to call himself a man ever again; for one of the bullets had ripped off his testicles. Yet only a few minutes before, this little boy was full of life, zest and energy, just like any other boy in this battle-torn village on the banks of the Niger River. A short while ago, he was playing and running about gaily on the green fields, chasing grasshoppers in the glorious West African sunset, killing time and waiting for his mama to call out when supper was ready, to call out that it was time to quit playing in the fields and come home because his daddy, the peasant wine-tapper, was already home, exhausted and starving as usual. But what the playing little boy did not realise was that the 'Nigerian' and 'Biafran' armies were closing in silently on both sides. Suddenly he was caught in the crossfire and, the next moment, he was dead.

This is not a happy story. But the saddest thing is not the manner of the boy's death, or that he died young, or even that he died at all. The real tragedy is that he died without knowing why. And in this, he was not alone. Hundreds of other children suffered the same fate that same day all over the country, just as others did the day before and many more would surely do on the morrow. What's more, starving and over-exploited peasants who had been dragooned into the emergency armies with drummed-up emotions, were being slaughtered in thousands between every sunrise and sunset with weapons made in Birmingham, Coventry and Moscow, the lamentable fact still being that they were all dying without a clue why. These poor people, the murdered children, the raped and butchered women, the brutalised and slaughtered peasants, all deserve an obituary at a proper time and place which, if I know myself, will probably never get written. My immediate concern here is to indict their murderers, the same people who murdered Nigeria, the murderers of our great country at a time when every sixth African was a Nigerian, the murderers of a country which, by virtue of numbers, economic potential, richness of culture and the shere inertia of the rest of Africa, was in a unique position to change the history of Africa and, through a united powerful Africa, the history of the world.

In case I have created the wrong impression, I want to make it clear at the outset that I do not resent the fact that blood is flowing in Nigeria. What I regret is that the *wrong* blood is flowing in that country. I do not lament the fact that people are being killed. It is inevitable that blood will flow in Nigeria. My contention is that it ought to be the blood of the guilty, who in spite of what some of us would like to believe, are not the 'savage Hausas' or the 'dominating Ibos' or any other particular tribal group we want to blame for lack of better explanation for our frustration. The guilty ones are those 'smart Alecs'—and no tribe has a monopoly of them—who, in the interest of their pockets and political self-glorification, collectively and relentlessly murdered Nigeria and, before this, used the same Nigeria as a weapon to stab at African Unity at Monrovia and, more recently, used the misguided Hausa peasants as an agrarian guillotine to mutilate and murder thirty thousand Ibos and trigger off the holocaust now going on in the country. This very clique have persistently and successfully fooled the whole of Nigeria into always apportioning blame to anyone but themselves and when, at last, history threatened to catch up with them and expose them for what they were, they shamelessly sacrificed the lives of thirty thousand people and countless others just to save their own necks.

In the midst of the confusion, they have mostly fled the very country they have plunged into turmoil, running from one foreign country to another, making speeches and assuming the ambivalent role of de-tribalised tribal negotiators overseas, claiming to be the champions and heroes of the very people they have betrayed. No doubt they will all survive the war as they survived the death of Nigeria while millions of innocent peasants perish. No. It is about time someone spoke up. It is about time we stopped the mass immolation of penniless peasants, whatever is left of them. It is about time the masses were told the truth. It is about time we found out what is really wrong with our long-plagued society for we have blamed the wrong people too long, too often, too gullibly.

First, we blamed the imperialist White devil alone and, getting rid of the White governor, we replaced him with the Black politician. Then we blamed the Black politician and, beheading the Prime Minister, we supplanted him with a Military Overlord and, getting rid of him, we have put tribal governors on thrones of bayonets.

One day, we were hailing Tafawa, 'the golden voice of Nigeria', and the very next day we celebrated the news that his 'golden' throat had been slit open. We cheered 'Ironsides' at the approach of Ironsi and, with the echo of our hosanna still ringing in the air, we highlifed at the news that iron pellets had crashed into his skull. We have shifted ground so much so often that the old 'corrupt' politicians whom we jubilantly swept away are right back into power again both in 'Nigeria' and 'Biafra' where, as shadow governments, they are now running the country to doom once again, raising regional military governors as a puppeteer a puppet, globe-trotting on our money all over again on 'fact-finding missions'. Is it really possible that our memory is so short-lived or have we become so blind that we cannot see that our point of arrival has coincided with our original point of departure? We have killed, maimed, brutalised and dehumanised countless numbers of our countrymen, first for being on the 'wrong' side of our politics, and then for being born on the 'wrong' side of the Niger. We have even disembowelled pregnant women and scalpelled unborn babies as the cure to our national ills. Yet the problems of Nigeria remain unsolved. Why?

This is the question I shall attempt briefly to tackle here. The trouble is that when, in the past, I came out with frank and unbiased articles on this subject, my critics called me an idealist. But history has proved, I regret to say, that far from being an idealist, I was only a realist in a crowd of biased pseudo-idealists.

When the news of the massacre of the Ibos in the North first hit the headlines, I was probably the only Ibo alive who did not feel like rushing into the street and killing every Hausa man in sight. I cared sufficiently for those dead victims to realise that frothing indignation was too simple an answer for such a grave problem. I have exposed myself to many scathing experiences in my time and have come to learn, at a great price, that at moments of crisis people are apt to resort to emotionalism when only cold-blooded application of reason is apt. Most people take refuge in emotionalism because it makes the least demand on one's intelligence and manhood.

It is always easier to beat one's breast heartily and blame others for a citadel of infamy than to employ one's inner powers and knock down that citadel to erect a better one in its place with hammer, hoe and bullet, as opposed to Cadillac, sky-scrapers and Anglo-Saxon academic degrees which produce intellectuals when Africa needs intelligent men. But apart from the argument that emotion is a poor substitute for reason when it comes to the real crunch, I have become very suspicious of emotionalists of late; for in recent Nigerian experience, it has proved that they often mean individualism when they talk about patriotism, personal aggrandisement when they talk about national property and the pursuit of justice.

The first thing that strikes anyone seeking an explanation for the Nigerian crisis today is that many explanations have already been churned out by many Western 'experts' and professional 'friends' of Nigeria, some conflicting, a good many so revoltingly off the mark that these attempts to explain the Nigerian confusion have, in themselves, become part of the confusion; and the only thing that becomes increasingly apparent is the intellectual wishful thinking behind these 'expert' analyses, not to mention the vested interests behind the friendliness of the professional 'friends' of Africa. Therefore, to avoid pouring new wine into old

G

skin, it will be best to begin this analysis of the Nigerian situation by clearing away these old cobwebs, disposing of the negative theories and the patronising explanations that have so far confused rather than elucidated and inflamed rather than abated the crisis.

First, we find the blue-eyed 'Africans', south of the Zambezi, pointing gleefully at Nigeria, and then at the Congo and other areas of political unrest in Africa, as proofs of the African's inherent inability to govern himself; but since this has an undertone of fascism and is so ridiculously wrong anyway, I prefer to treat it with the contempt it deserves, hoping that the day is not far off when the Blacks of Southern Africa will turn this White daydream of race superiority into a nightmare.

The most propagated explanation, and that which unfortunately most Nigerians are in fact beginning to echo, is that Nigerian disintegration is a result of a miscalculated attempt to make one nation out of many culturally irreconcilable tribal 'nations', a theory which of course not only applies to other African states but, above all, makes nonsense of the concept of Pan-Africanism. And, to lend substance to this theory, a number of African scholars, reading sociology in Western Universities, are being co-opted and given grants to research into and specialise in specific tribal characteristics—not group similarities, but their peculiarities, the cultural distinctness of each tribal group as opposed to the others. Further, some Western-acclaimed literary giants of Africa, especially of Nigeria, are successfully encouraged to expend their literary talents on singing and extolling the exclusive glories of different tribes to the point where the conclusion must be that the Ibos, the Hausas and the Yorubas are so ethnically irreconcilable that it is impossible for them to live together as one country. One well known writer, for instance, makes a living out of attacking Nkrumah and his Pan-African idea consistently in his plays: and, not content with that, he ridicules Senghor's Negritude by calling it 'tigritude'. No wonder he is the Nigerian literary wonder-boy on the Western pop-literature chart. I mention this, even at the risk of being called jealous, to point out that

the Tshombes of African literature are more destructive than
the Tshombes of African politics because the scar they leave
on the African personality is on the brain, not on the heart,
much deeper, more long-lasting and less detectable. So
advanced is the Western science of imagery, perfected over
the centuries, that, at a time when Africa should be producing, and can produce, her own Dostoyevskies, Chekhovs,
Gorkies and more Leroi Joneses, this science of image-
manipulation has been used successfully to control the
African literary scene so effectively that a bunch of reactionary literary zombies are being brought to the fore as the
best we can offer, and used as weapons to carve up our
beloved country into tribal Bantustans at a time when all
Africa is thirsting for unity. It is sad. It is even sadder that
Western 'experts' decree the Hausa the traditional enemy
of the Ibo, which, in translation, means that the Hausa is
the mortal enemy of the Ibo, and, on further translation,
means that the Hausa is the deadliest enemy of the Ibo, and
progressively, has come to mean that you cannot have national
unity granted the presence of tribal and cultural diversities.

What makes this conclusion laughable is that the same
explanation has been offered by the same Western 'experts'
for the separation of India and Pakistan, even though the
Indian Bengali has much more in common with the Pakistani
Bengali than he does with the Indian Punjabi.

And what is even more noteworthy is that these 'experts',
who use the cultural 'differences' of African tribes as a basis
for forecasting the doom of African states, are usually proud
citizens of a country like the United States of America, where
all the tribes under the sun, all the races under the sun, all
the religions under the sun, and all the cultures of entire
mankind have been brought together to live under one flag.

They also talk about Nigeria being too populous to be
a single nation, and once again conveniently forget that the
two most powerful nations of the world, the United States
and the Soviet Union, have become what they are today
primarily because each derives her strength from populations
of well over two hundred million peoples of diversified
ethnic and cultural backgrounds, and the result has been

a bigger nation with a richer culture. More significantly they never tell us that a quarter of the earth's population now lives under one flag in China and, because of this, China, only a few years ago ridiculed in the West as 'a heap of sand' and 'the sick man of East Asia', has utilised her enormous manpower to rise from obscurity to become today an indisputable power factor in world diplomacy.

And yet, our 'experts' have been forcing it down my throat since I was a pre-fertilised egg-cell that an under-populated territory like Nigeria, with barely fifty million people, all of whom have been rampaged by a common exploiter, all of whom have drunk deep of the waters of alien capitalist affliction, all of whom worked side by side to build up the economies and greatness of other lands, cannot now live side by side to build up their own. Surely no Black man in his right senses can be expected to carry innocence to such a point of folly as to swallow such erroneous analysis.

From the above brief examination, it may easily be seen that none of the explanations offered by the 'experts' for the trouble in Nigeria holds water.

There is one very important fact that the chaos of Nigeria has exposed. This fact is that Independence is not negotiable. True Independence cannot be secured by constitution talks. How can you sit down at a table with your oppressor and ask him to tell you how best to get rid of himself? Unless he is an extremely foolish man, which no colonial power is or can afford to be, the best he can do is to give you a rope to hang yourself and save himself the trouble of doing the dirty job himself. That is precisely what has happened in Nigeria. We have gone to the very oppressor we want to get rid of, and after telling him our plans in full and in beautiful English, asked him to give us the secret of his greatness so that we can grow stronger than he is and then destroy him. And of course, he listened to us patiently and offered to teach us all about Independence. The trouble is he has taught us all about Independence, except what Independence is and how to achieve it. This may be laughable, but it is exactly what has happened, not only in Nigeria but in the whole of Africa. While we are beating drums and celebrating

Independence, the whole world is laughing its head off. It is about time our people realised that history is a dictionary of human experiences. When a man is reading a book and comes across a key word he does not understand, there is only one thing for him to do. He must lay the book aside, turn to a dictionary, search out the meaning of the problem word, and only then can he come back to his book, properly equipped to read on, grasp and digest the wisdom in the pages ahead. The same applies to life in general. When we find ourselves involved in the book of life and come across a dilemma, whether as an individual, a race, a nation, an oppressed minority or even a revolutionary group, the intelligent thing to do is first to search through that dictionary of human experiences called history and, when we find out how other peoples have resolved problems similar to ours in the past, then we can, with intelligent adaptation, tackle the one in hand according to the inexorable laws of history. This, to me, is the fundamental use of history. Without it, history becomes meaningless, just an accumulation of fairy tales at best for the amusement of intellectual masturbators or, as is more often the case, a propaganda gift to the colonialist who, far from seeking to explain the past, thrives on distorting it to justify the atrocious present. Therefore, used, as it should be, as an encyclopaedia of man's resolutions of problems, history, to a people in search of an answer, is like a map to a lost traveller. But because the African leaders have failed to do this, they now find themselves receiving 'independence' when they should be taking power, going west when they should go east, thrusting out umbrellas when it is dry, disintegrating when they should integrate, eating lard when palm-oil would suffice, preaching birth-control when Africa is underpopulated, begging capital to employ labour when it is labour that employs capital, being reactive when they should be active, being imitators when, if they must, they should be emulators and, above all, licking the bums of dirty-arsed foreign buccaneers who have sat down first on the African economy and now on the African mentality.

History is full of examples of peoples who have made

revolutions before our time. What we should have done before embarking on our own was to learn from the experiences of those other peoples the true meaning of revolution, all the implications of revolution and the inexorable historical laws which every revolution must obey to succeed. Let us take just a few examples as analysed by the late Brother Malcolm. The American revolution of 1776 has two significant characteristics. First, it was based on a struggle for land and, secondly, it was secured by violence. The French Revolution, by the landless against the landlords, has the same two significant characteristics. It was based on a struggle for land and secured by violence. The Russian Revolution of 1917, by the landless against the landlords, has those two significant characteristics. It was based on a struggle for land and secured by violence. The Chinese Revolution, a revolution which has elevated eight hundred million people from a state of laughing-stock backwardness and economic slavery to become an industrial superpower and a force to be reckoned with in world diplomacy, also has the two significant characteristics. It was a revolution firstly based on a struggle for land and secondly secured by bloodshed. The Cuban Revolution has the same characteristics again, and today the Vietnamese masses too are fighting for their freedom in accordance with the historical laws of revolution.

I cite these examples to show that a revolution, to be a revolution, must inevitably have two requirements. First, it must be aimed at the change of ownership and control of the means of production, e.g. land. Secondly, it can be secured only by violence. Put differently, a successful revolution is one in which the ownership and control of the sources of wealth in the land have been taken over by the people for whom the revolution is made and, since no group surrenders power to another peacefully, there is no such thing as a peaceful revolution. A revolution is made when a people discover, as may soon be the case in South Africa, that they have been deprived too long and will not be allowed by the status quo to live as men till they are ready to die and kill as men.

The only peaceful revolution in history, the one exception to the rule, is the African 'revolution'. The only revolution based on constitutional talks is the African 'revolution'. The only revolution where the worthiness of the leaders of revolution is based on knighthoods and academic titles conferred by the very people whose values the revolution is out to destroy is, yes, the African 'revolution'. Is it any wonder that African Independence today is no more than a nickname?

This is the number one thing the Nigerian crisis has brought into the open. True Independence can never come from the corridors of Whitehall. How can it? Can milk flow out of the 'breasts' of a bird?

While on violence and revolution, I want to state immediately that violence is just as repulsive to me as it is to the next man. But unlike most people, I do not call violence violence only when it suits me. It is very difficult for many intellectual liberals to understand that violence is not always accompanied by the boom of guns and the clatter of bayonets. When a little African boy is compelled to die of starvation in a world where there is abundancy, I call it violence. When an old Black man in Harlem is made by his fellow men to live all his days sharing dingy tenements with rats, I call that violence. When I see that Africa is the richest continent in the world and Africans are the poorest people on the same planet, I call that violence. When the American Jemez Indian is rounded up like an animal in pueblo reservations with hardly any room to lay a sleeping blanket, I call it violence. When I see fifteen-year-old Black girls in San Francisco reduced to a state of want where they have to peddle sex for bare survival, I call that violence. And nearer home, when I see that the leather of my English landlord's shoes could be from my home, the material of his clothes mine, the stick of his rolled umbrella mine, the gold of his wife's jewelry mine, the copper of his cigarette-case and the tobacco in it too mine, when I see all this and that even the manganese of his industry and the oil that runs the machines are all from my home, while my own mother, a woman who, judging by the standards of her faraway English dependants, should be living like a queen, is indeed living on the hunger line, I call that violence. In short, in a world where two people out of three are suffering want, starvation and death just to appease the pockets of a born-to-be-rich minority, I call it a hell of violence. It is reactionary violence of the worst kind, and if it requires revolutionary violence to vanquish it and allow starving millions to eat and give children in the womb of time a chance to survive, I am all for revolutionary violence. Christianity paved the way for imperialism by teaching Africans that violence is wrong. They conveniently failed to distinguish between reactionary violence, which is offensive, and revolutionary violence, which is defensive. And today, the liberal Whites have taken over where the White missionaries left off, telling me how horrified by violence they all are and going straight home to switch on their television sets to be entertained by violence. They are either lying to themselves or trying to fool me as they once fooled and destroyed my father. I don't think they are lying to themselves. The Nigerian lied to himself when he thought that Independence comes peacefully. Now he is paying for it. What he may not know is that the price he has paid so far is chicken-feed in comparison to things to come—unless he acts *now*.

Another glaring fact emerges from the Nigerian situation. The elimination of Tafawa, as I pointed out briefly above, has not eliminated the national dilemma it was supposed to eliminate. On the contrary, many 'Nigerians' and 'Biafrans' believe that Nigeria under Tafawa was a happier country than the Nigeria of today. In other words, the change of leadership has not improved the situation at all. In spite of the successive leaderships introduced, one after another, to change conditions for the better, the situation has in fact worsened. One can only conclude from this that what is wrong with Nigeria is not really the leadership as we have always thought, but the one thing which has always remained constant while the leaderships were changing. And that is: the *system* under which the various leaderships tried to operate. And they could only fail. Even if a band of angels had been sent down from heaven to lead Nigeria, they too would have failed, as long as that system remained unchanged. This is the key to the Nigerian crisis today. Until that is understood, a revived Nigeria is a pipe-dream, so also a durable 'Biafra'. Until this fact is taken into consideration and a new mass-based society founded under a proper ideological system, we are building a national edifice on a volcano; and all those who think we have tribal problems today will come to realise too late they haven't seen a thing yet.

In the interest of those who might think that I am now just getting wise after the event, I want to state at this point that, as far back as 1962, I wrote a series of articles which ran in many leading African papers. And in those articles, I put forward the very arguments I am advancing here now and even predicted, correct to the nearest date of their eruption, the calamities which were about to befall Nigeria. I cried out from my soul about the terrible days ahead just as I am crying out now about the disasters yet to explode.

In the *West African Pilot* on Thursday, July 12, 1962, I stated:

The cure for tribalism is ideological leadership. A political ideology does not correspond with tribal, geographical or religious units. It cuts across barriers and induces unity. I do not pretend that the universal introduction of ideological leadership into Africa means the complete absence of differences of opinion. I do assert, however, that the differences of opinion created by ideological leadership tend to unite rather than divide a people because they make it possible for the Ibo man to agree with his Hausa brother even though he disagrees with his own blood brother at home and vice versa.

I went on to explain that

the colonialists see to it that before granting independence to a people, they condition those people to regard independence simply as the freedom to decide *who* is to govern instead of *how* to be governed, which comes first. They ensure that the colonised people are made to put *who* before *how*. The result is that African politics have become the politics of personalities instead of the politics of ideologies. The fire of personality politics has invariably been stoked into tribal and regional barren controversies. And who gains from it all? The foreign capitalist who, from time immemorial, has found the 'divide and rule' policy a handy means for sending his exploiting tentacles into African economic life.

On corruption, I pointed out:

Another obvious advantage of mass understanding of political ideology is its tendency to eliminate corruption. People will then vote for ideology they believe in instead of just voting for the presently fashionable man who can bribe them most, sometimes with money from abroad. A man who votes for a political party which he knows to profess a capitalist system can hardly be expected to complain when the MP whom he has thus voted into power utilises his portfolio to amass wealth for himself in order to keep society capitalist. On the other hand, a man who votes for a socialist administration has at least the constitutional right to demand the dismissal of any MP who displays selfish and corrupt capitalist tendencies.

The frustrating mistake of Nigeria therefore was to expect a socialist morality in a capitalist economy. It didn't work, does not work, and can never work because

any African country that fails to define its ideological stance based on a nation-wide mass-revolutionary mandate will have to grapple with nebulous and unpredictable policies to the discredit of the electorate. Any country which has no clear-cut ideological objective can only dream about a salutary future. Going back to the simile of the ship, such country has no destination. It has no leadership and no captain but just an adventuring group of political pirates who are prepared to prey on and plunder their crew when no enemy ship is in sight.

Nigerians are still paying the price of this plunder with blood, sweat and unspeakable misery.

But it was in the *Daily Express* of Wednesday, October 10, 1962, that I tried to set the Nigerian problem within a simplified, clear and understandable historical framework. The idea was to give our people a simple device by which to gauge not only what was happening in Nigeria at the time but also how it was related to what was happening in other parts of Africa and the world in general, to enable them to predict the future and forestall any adverse political contingency. This device was to divide the recent political history of Africa into two main phases which I called BG and AG, meaning 'Before the emergence of Ghana' and 'After the emergence of Ghana' respectively.

I need not go into the detailed analysis of the circumstances, remote and immediate, which led to African 'independence'. All that is necessary here is to recollect that at a certain time in the history of post-war Africa, a point was reached when the colonial powers were compelled by a combination of various historical forces to agree to negotiate 'independence' with peoples of their colonies. It is important to remember that this was not a voluntary decision and that the colonial powers had then, as now, no intention of leaving Africa. All they intended doing was to grant the colonial peoples an illusion of independence, to grant them token independence, haul down the Union Jack and haul it up again in unrecognisable patterns, write the 'savages' a new National Anthem with tom-tom backings as long as the kids sang it in scout uniforms, recall home the White governor and replace him with a Black 'tentacle' of White imperialism and then christen the British Empire a Commonwealth in which the wealth is of course not common.

They dared not, however, grant this sambo 'independence' to all African countries at once. Things might get out of hand. They had to experiment first with a country not large enough to constitute a serious headache if the plan went wrong and, at the same time, the people of this little country must be sufficiently 'educated' and Westernised to buy the Western 'democratic' ideas as a matter of course. Gold Coast qualified on both counts and, as we all know, came to be the first guinea-pig country to be given 'independence'.

But in choosing Gold Coast, the imperialists had made a serious mistake. They had forgotten that Gold Coast had a man called Nkrumah. The first thing Kwame did was to kill Gold Coast and resurrect a Ghana that would soon rock the world. He declared that the independence of Ghana was meaningless until the whole of Africa was free. On the domestic front, he generated an economic and industrial revolution at a pace which even dumbfounded his critics and, on the world political scene, he became the Lenin of his era and the thumping pulse of an uncompromising Pan-African revolution. Above all, he made his people realise that the first act of political independence was to choose *how* they wanted to be governed because it was this which would determine *who* was best qualified to be employed as a political leader to carry it out.

Accordingly, he went to the people and, in a national referendum, the people of Ghana decided resoundingly that *how* they wanted to be governed was along the road to socialism and that *whom* they entrusted this job to was the CPP under the leadership of Osagyefo Kwame Nkrumah. They decided overwhelmingly that capitalism must be destroyed to give way to socialism, and that any traitors who stood in the way must be thrown into the house of correction. All over the Black world, Kwame Nkrumah became a name to conjure with and a revolutionary source of inspiration and pride to his oppressed Black brothers in America who, whether in the ghettoes of Harlem or in Vine City, Atlanta, whether boiling in the racist cauldron of the North or wading through the Klan-ridden hell of the South, are no longer the history-less African-hating sambos of the past, no longer the ever-supplicating American of yesterday, but a hyphenated American, the Afro-American who now understands the economic aspects of racism in ideological terms but, even more, sees the extension of Pan-Africanism to worldwide Pan-Blackism as the logical answer to international imperialist White Power. Ghana became the Olympus of Black revolution and the Mecca of Black revolutionaries while the

Osagyefo of Ghana himself became the uncontested redeemer of the Black psyche the world over.

This was more than the colonial powers bargained for. If tiny Ghana with a population of seven million and only one Nkrumah could create such a tremor, what was going to happen, they wondered, if even mightier 'Ghanas' were to erupt like shattering volcanoes in the then independence-seeking countries like Nigeria, with a teeming population of forty million and many potential 'Nkrumahs' like Zik and budding socialist hawks in the leadership?

The mere thought of this scared the pants off the imperialist 'freedom-givers'. And from then onwards, it became clear that a new era had begun, the 'AG' era in which a completely new strategy was to be applied to all countries that got their 'independence' after Ghana. Africans were no longer to be allowed to pick their own leaders. Instead puppet governments must be imposed on African countries as a condition of 'independence'. Democracy was no longer to mean a people's democracy but an out-and-out 'puppet-ocracy'; and the emphasis shifted, as in Kikuyu-strong Kenya, from the sanctity of the majority voice to the protection of minority interests. From then onwards, as I pointed out in an article in the *West African Pilot* of Friday, July 13, 1962, 'many an Independence-Eve Constitutional Conference in London has proved a provision for the imperialist auctioneer to strike his diplomatic mallet after selling political power to whichever African leader bids highest in sycophancy.'

That was precisely what happened in Nigeria. Nigeria was the first victim of this new imperialist 'AG' strategy. To make sure Nigeria did not become strong and powerful like Ghana, seeds of disunity were sown everywhere and an unworkable constitution given her as a basis for national construction and 'independence'. It is most surprising, looking back at that constitution, that Nigeria lasted as long as it did because the neo-colonialist did his arithmetic well and saw to it that that constitution was unworkable anywhere, even in heaven.

A new bourgeoisie was created to anglicise Nigeria to the

point of anathematising socialism. They fooled everyone in Nigeria that all was well at a time when society was disintegrating, corruption rampant, the gap between the rich and the poor widening and the country careering to inevitable doom. This was what Arthur Helliwell, a British reporter whom one can hardly accuse of being a communist agitator, wrote about the capital of Nigeria in *The People* of Sunday, August 23, 1964:

> This is a city of vivid, violent and often vastly disturbing contrasts. It is a city where soaring skyscrapers tower over acres of squalid shanty-town slums. A city in which the dividing line between the very rich and the very poor is sharp and shocking. Outside expensive, air-conditioned restaurants serving caviare, lobster, steaks and fine French wines, maimed and blind beggars plead for alms in the damp heat. Cabinet ministers purr through the slums in their free Mercedes and Cadillac limousines to their £50,000 homes in the Hollywood atmosphere of Ikowi. Tribal chiefs from upcountry, magnificently robed in gold thread fabrics, smile and nod over vodka martinis in luxurious bars sealed against the stench from the city's notorious open drains. And you can hail a taxi outside the towering and beautiful new Independence Building, as modern as tomorrow, and, within an hour, drive into a frightening land of Ju Ju and witchcraft as old as time— few ordinary working-class Nigerians are any better off today than they were under the British—for the poor, life is a bare existence. On £3 a week a labourer supports not only his family but a host of relatives. At the other end of the scale government ministers and top civil servants earn £20-a-week running allowance and free mansions with no telephone or electricity bills. Even ordinary MPs are pampered. They all get good jobs out-side politics, are paid £1,000 a year for working one month out of twelve, live in free luxury flats on Victoria Island and have generous car allowances. But the real maggot in the apple is the fat canker of corruption that is eating into the heart of Nigeria. 'Dash' is the West

African slang for a bribe, and Nigeria has always been known as the Land of Dash. Politicians, police and civil servants are lining their pockets with bribes. And some have acquired enormous fortunes. I have been shown office blocks and apartment buildings worth hundreds of thousands of pounds, built with 'dash' money and owned by prominent public men. At least two politicians are said to have more than a million pounds in Swiss banks. Other corrupt officials have transferred fortunes to London and New York. Another top civil servant has converted his 'dash' into gold bars. Another man—a building contractor—said: 'In my trade, unless you are prepared to pay dash you might as well go out of business.' And yet another—Mark 10 Jaguar, gold cigarette case and suits tailored in Rome—confessed: 'Only fools are honest in Nigeria, today. And I can't afford to be a fool—'

Who now is the fool? History has proved beyond question that the real fool was that man who imagined that this state of affairs could last long. The real villains were all those who capitalised on the Nigerian 'dash' economy. It is evident today to the point of sadness that it was at the time when these things were happening in that country that the foundation for the murder of thirty thousand Ibos was being laid, and that everyone, directly or indirectly, Hausa or Ibo, who partook of the 'dash' dividends was as guilty of the Ibo genocide as the Kanuri who disembowelled a thousand pregnant Ibo women. I know many friends in London today whose education has been paid for with 'dash' money and they are the first to drive in luxurious autos to every one of their many 'patriotic' meetings to froth righteous indignation and blame the 'murderous' Hausas, or the 'Yamili' or 'Kobo-kobo' Ibos as the case may be, for ruining our 'peaceful and prosperous' Nigeria. When will they ever learn? When will they ever learn that the Ibo massacre was not the cause of Nigeria's ruin, but only a result of it, just one of the many symptoms of the mass frustrations long endured by every member of our peasant class? When will they ever learn that any society where the groan of the oppressed is as shattering as the oppressor's autos cannot last long? Nigeria, it was plain, was poised for explosion. It was a matter of time. The one person who knew this was a young man called Major Chukwuma Nzeogwu. He saw the writing on the wall, made himself an instrument of fate, and struck like a tornado. Nzeogwu's January coup of 1966 was more than a coup, it was a people's revolution. The jubilation of the masses, from Brass to Katsina, from Bamenda to Port Novo, and from the bare-breasted akara-vendor in Onitsha Market to the blind gworo-chewing beggar in the streets of Yola, was evidence of this. It was unfortunate, as Nzeogwu himself pointed out on the verge of tears later, that his colleagues did a bad job in the South because of 'incompetence and misguided considerations at the eleventh hour,' and thereby giving the coup, to the glory of the enemies of a formidable socialist Nigeria, a tribal outlook. I believe Nzeogwu, as I am sure many people did, when he said that 'tribal considerations were completely out of our minds.' I am convinced that that coup was not an attempt at a tribal take-over, but a well-timed socialist revolution, a coup masterminded and executed by a young major who had his finger on the pulse of the suffocating masses and knew when to strike, a young man who understood the ideological and neo-colonialist implications of Nigerian problems, a young hawk who had discovered that any society in which economic power is in the hands of the minority, especially a foreign-installed puppet minority, cannot be a civilisation but a jungle in which any talk of mass improvement can only be a pipe-dream. I am certain that Nzeogwu's revolutionary mission was to smash this mass-dehumanising system and that the masses wanted him to succeed. They wanted him to succeed because they knew that a young man bright enough to shatter the formidable CIA and British Intelligence networks overnight in the Nigeria of those days, was more than bright enough to carry through a socialist revolution and its programme in a country thirsting desperately for change.

This was the position when in stepped Major General Johnson Thomas Umunakwe Aguiyi-Ironsi, OFR, KBE, etc

etc etc. I hate to decry the dead but with a name like that Ironsi, poor fellow, was hardly the material for spear-heading a crashing socialist revolutionary programme. In the first place, he did not understand the ideological depth of the problem. Secondly, he could not even see the BG-AG strategy which led to the deposition of the puppet regime in Nigeria. And because he could not understand this, he failed to appreciate that the significance of Major Nzeogwu's coup was that, for the first time in the history of Black Africa, the people, under the leadership of the revolutionary wing of the army, had destooled a puppet neo-colonialist government imposed on them by a departing imperialist master. Had he realised that, he would have known that what had to be done at once was to consolidate power speedily in the hands of the people through a crashing socialist programme protected by a people's militia before the imperialists could hit back. Instead, Ironsi decided to rule by 'goodwill'. He took the imperialist flatterers too seriously and actually believed himself to be 'Ironsides' and the 'Strong man' when he was in fact an administrative weakling who surrounded himself with the wrong advisers who were not only untrustworthy, but mediocre and unintelligent as well. He stupidly and unnecessarily introduced the Decree 34 to nullify the federal constitution and establish a unitary government and failed to realise that no government could be unitary and survive in an economic system which compels disunity. He could not see that it was not a piece of paper which needed tearing, but an entire system which needed smashing and reconstructing. Worst of all, he did not see that the imperialists were arming for a come-back.

The imperialists had every cause to worry. They had suffered a shocking set-back. If a strong socialist government were to emerge in Nigeria, the tendency might have been to join forces with Nkrumah's Ghana and, with Sekou Toure's Guinea not too far away, who knows what the history of Africa might have been? With the mighty Nigeria, before now the toughest and most effective opposition to Nkrumah's socialist African Union Government, actually going over to the anti-imperialist Nkrumah-led camp, who

H

knows what might have happened?

The imperialists certainly did not wait to find out. It was soon clear they were up to something. Soon the American Peace Corps boys and girls, the junior CIA, were flooding the Northern Nigerian towns and villages in staggering numbers. Researching 'anthropologists' and holidaying 'professors' poured into every corner of the North under the grant's of the US government to 'work on' the villagers.

They tumbled in and out of bed with the top boys in the army and influential civilians and, very soon, the news soon spread that the January coup was an 'Ibo conspiracy'. First it began as a rumour and then it became common 'knowledge' that the Ibos and Hausas were mortal enemies.

In the East, meanwhile, the American junior CIA was also at work. The Peace Corps boys and girls peddled sex for propaganda from one university dormitory to another and from village to village. Soon the Ibos began to echo ideas thus implanted in their heads by their professional American 'lovers'. Everywhere they credited the January coup to the inherent Ibo genius. They boasted of being the 'Jews of Africa', an expression first used by *Time* Magazine five years ago, and of being 'capitalist by nature', and openly used self-flattering, meaningless and arrogant expressions auto-suggested to them during unguarded moments of Peace Corps sex orgies, expressions coined in America deliberately to exacerbate the non-Ibos. Soon what began as a miraculous non-tribal January revolution led by a brilliant and socialist-willed young major was soon whittled down, abused, demeaned and fanned into a petty inter-tribal vendetta. We all know what this led to. The tragedy was that the men who had thrown Major Nzeogwu into jail in order to 'correct his mistake' and 'appease the Northerners' could neither cope with the situation nor appease anyone.

I was in Atlanta, Georgia, when I heard that a second coup had taken place in Nigeria and that a certain Yakubu Gowon was now in power. My first reaction was joy because I had rather optimistically thought that my secret hope had come true. I had thought that Gowon was another angry young revolutionary of Nzeogwu's ideological orientation and that he had swept Ironsi out of power in order to take over control and carry on from where Nzeogwu left off. I did not care one peanut which tribe he came from and still don't. All that was important to me was that he 'was the right man'. But it soon became obvious that I had counted my corn before the harvest. The first thing Gowon did was to declare a return to Tafawaism. It stung my ear like hearing an assistant on a rescue-raft pushing his captain overboard half-way to the shore and then declaring an immediate about-turn and a return to the deck of the sinking ship from which the crew were originally rescued. The more I listened to Gowon, the more convinced I became that the only time this man talked sense was not thinking. The real limit came when he proposed the division of Nigeria into twelve regions as a solution to the chaos created by dividing Nigeria into only three regions.

It was not long before I realised that, far from what I thought at first, Gowon's counter-coup was a neo-colonialist come-back, that Gowon was an Uncle Tom brainwashed by the imperialists to do with a bayonet what Tafawa could not do with a golden voice. The effect was to return a pro-Western puppet administration to power in Nigeria and therefore seal the doom of socialism for good in this key part of Africa, keep Nigeria weak and divided so that, while Nigerians are busy killing each other, the real victors will be those foreigners who are capitalising from selling the two sides weapons of destruction, not to mention the £1,000-a-week White mercenary pilots and the fascist White regimes of Southern Africa who are speedily consolidating their forces **and** pushing northwards on both military and diplomatic fronts to take over Africa a second time. Thanks to Gowon and Ankrah, West Africa is fast becoming the Black Man's Grave.

I watched Ojukwu's emergence with interest and even concealed hope. I had known Ojukwu as far back as my secondary-school days at Nnewi. I respected his intellect and liked him as a man, except of course that he read far more Shakespeare than was good for a Pan-Africanist. I knew that if anyone could trounce Gowon and his neo-colonialist masters the Nzeogwu way, that man was Ojukwu. He had the brains, the international respect, the hardihood and the charisma. Ojukwu was in a unique position to carry the whole of Nigeria with him.

But he made one tragic mistake. He allowed himself to be swayed too much by his understandably emotional followers. By declaring himself for 'Biafra' and 'Biafra' only, he put himself in exactly the same mould as Gowon. It is true that all the arguments are in his favour. Until recently, the Ibos were the most anxious tribe to create a Unified Nigeria. The NCNC, led by Dr Azikiwe, an Ibo, was for a United Nigeria and tried to operate as a national party. It is true that the Action Group started in the West as primarily a party of Yorubas, an essentially tribalistic party. It is true that, in the North, the feudal rulers formed the Northern Peoples Congress on an entirely tribal basis, forcing regional constitution on Nigeria after making themselves an embarrassing impediment to 'independence' negotiations. It is true that, on the social level, the Ibos lived in Nigeria as Nigerians, travelling, working and settling down in all parts of the country without distinction. It is true also that they lost 30,000 of their kin and that Gowon literally forced secession on Ojukwu by dividing Nigeria into twelve states.

These arguments are sound and unanswerable. But the fact remains that Ojukwu should have asked himself what he really wanted and how best to achieve it. If he had, I doubt if he would have considered 'Biafra for the Biafrans' the wisest way of achieving it. He listened to advisers who, evidently, saw Nigeria as a state in a vacuum. His advisers, like the advisers of many other military governments in Africa, failed to see that there are other powerful forces at work in the world, forces whose torque and dimensions must be put into consideration while working out one's strategies.

What Ojukwu should have told the world was that he was not fighting the Hausas as such, but a neo-colonialist puppet military clique which happened to be Hausa. He should have declared himself the champion of, not only the Ibos, but all the have-nots and masses of that country who have suffered and will suffer under a puppet administration, military or civil. He could still have made 'Biafra' his base but the important thing was that he made it manifest that his was a non-tribal socialist revolution. Had he done this, Russia would have been too embarrassed to give military aid to Nigeria. In fact, Russia and all the socialist countries would have come out openly in support of Biafra, including China. He would have had everything to gain and nothing to lose. The progressive countries of Africa would have considered it their duty to recognise Biafra; and Ojukwu would have emerged from being the hounded lone 'rebel' he is today to become the Fidel Castro of a throbbing new African state. The 'traitors' who were shot for trying to get rid of Ojukwu and create a vacuum for socialism would have been alive today, fighting for a socialist 'Biafra'. And I, for one, instead of hibernating and writing revolutionary literature in this dingy tenement in London, would be right there in the 'jungles of Biafra', converting my philosophy into reality.

I am not asking Ojukwu to tell a lie to the peoples of the world in order to enlist their help to win a war. What I ask him is to tell what is after all the truth. It is not a lie that he is fighting a neo-colonialist military administration trying to impose a feudal puppet dictatorship on the over-exploited masses of Nigeria. All he had to do was to call this spade a spade and identify himself with those 'Biafrans' who have been the victim of it, as well as the 'non-Biafrans'. Because he has not taken this line, Gowon has out-manoeuvred him all the way, pulling both the socialist and non-socialist powers to his side and blackmailing the rest of the world into treating 'Biafra' with contempt. The way things are in the world today, the only way a country like 'Biafra' could convince anyone that her situation is not a domestic concern of a parent country like Nigeria alone is to cross the ideological carpet, forcing all countries who have a vested interest in her adopted ideology to see her fight as their fight as well and therefore recognise her sovereignty by words and deeds. We have seen it work in China, we have seen it in Cuba, we have seen it in Korea, and we are seeing it now in Vietnam. Why then is it impossible in 'Biafra'?

I can only think of two possible reasons why Ojukwu, a

'confirmed socialist', has not declared 'Biafra' a militant socialist state.

The first could be that such a declaration might upset his American 'friends' and jeopardise possible secret drippings of American 'aid' with which 'Biafra' could do at the moment. However, apart from the fact that such 'aid' is the same threadbare old American trick of blackmail, its acceptance is based on the far-fetched presumption that America is not 'aiding' the other side as well. It is an open secret that America has of late embarked upon a new strategy of moving in wherever there is conflict in Africa today to start 'aiding' the two opposing sides involved in the conflict, none of them any wiser of course that Sam is the enemy's uncle as well. A good example was in the Congo recently where the State Department was backing President Mobutu while the CIA was financing the White mercenaries invading his country. If this sounds crazy, a closer scrutiny soon reveals that Sam has indeed a method in his madness. It reveals that, with this method of backing the two sides, America can never lose. If 'Biafra' comes out triumphant in the end, Sam is the undisputed uncle. If 'Nigeria' wins, Sam also is the swell uncle. This way, America ensures that whatever is the verdict of battle, the field of battle itself remains within the American sphere of influence. If my hunch is right and this is the American game in 'Biafra' at the moment, I am obliged to say that it is extremely unwise of Ojukwu's advisers to pin their hopes on an uncle who is investing in their success as well as their failure. I state once again that the drippings of American or Israeli underground 'aid' which 'Biafra' might lose by going socialist is nothing compared to the flood of all-round open aid and military support which must flow into 'Biafra' from every corner of the earth where the red-hot steam-roller of socialism is crushing the people's oppressors out of existence. With this support, too, will come the inevitable recognition of 'Biafra' by those countries.

The second and, I think, the greatest impediment to 'Biafran' socialism today is, I am sure, Ojukwu's advisers themselves, and his ambassadors overseas. They are largely elite, the same old bunch of pseudo-intellectual zombies and

corrupt politicians who would rather blame the raping of
Nigeria on other people than on the decadent system which
they themselves helped to foster on the nation for pounds,
shillings and pence. They want a 'free Biafra' for the wrong
reasons because they do not share the same aspirations as
the masses. They tell the people of 'Biafra' today that 'we
must first keep our house in order' just as they once told
the people of a young Nigeria as an argument against African
Union Government that 'we must first keep our house in
order' before plunging the very 'house' they were supposed
to keep in order into disorder. 'Biafra' is a country created
to fight off oppression and, by its very existence, is committed
to a system that must be a negation of class oppression. That
is why Ojukwu, as a right leader of 'Biafra', must rid himself
of advisers who, as a class, are a contradiction of 'Biafra'. He
must surely know he has nothing whatever to lose. For the
first time in the history of our continent, a battle-brazened
people's militia has been formed and the people love him
to adoration. What revolutionary leader could ask for more?

If only to change the tide of military misfortunes in
'Biafra' and drive the invaders out, it is to the socialist camp
that the 'Biafran' leader must now turn. There is no other
way and, for reasons I would rather not go into here, I
know for certain it will work. I know it is not idealistic to
advise this, as it might seem to the crypto-Western cynics at
first. I repeat, it can work.

No doubt, Ojukwu's advisers will oppose this step with
the same degree of conviction, wisdom and air of infallibility
with which they once assured Ojukwu that 'Biafra' would
get universal recognition not longer than one second after
her secession. It has been one hell of a long second for
Ojukwu for accepting their 'educated' advice. Like Ironsi,
they are all sincere men I am sure, but this is the one game
where sincerity is not enough. They would decry socialism
as a 'foreign concept' even though they would be the first
to recommend Montesquieu's Separation of Powers and
Dicey's Rule of Law as the sine qua non of African political
survival. They would call it ignoble to 'collaborate with the
communists' who have committed the unforgivable crime of

fighting universal man's inhumanity to man but they would go to the foulest alleys of the world to bargain for the collaboration of White mercenaries whose bayonets are still crimson with the blood of Black Congolese babies. The truth of the matter is that the fear which most 'educated' Africans have for communism is not a rational fear at all, but a 'been-to-England' phobia inculcated into them by their colonial 'educators' during their student days in Europe and America. Dr Nkrumah described them beautifully in *Consciencism*:

Many of them had been hand-picked and, so to say, carried certificates of worthiness with them. These were considered fit to become enlightened servants of the colonial administration. The process by which this category of student became fit usually started at an early age, for not infrequently they had lost contact in early life with their traditional background. By reason of their lack of contact with their own roots, they became prone to accept some theory of universalism, provided it was expressed in vague, mellifluous terms. Armed with their universalism, they carried away from their university courses an attitude entirely at variance with the concrete reality of their people and their struggle. When they come across doctrines of a combative nature, like those of Marxism, they reduced them to arid abstractions, to common-room subtleties. In this way, through the good graces of their colonialist patrons, these students, now competent in the art of forming not a concrete environmental view of social problems, but an abstract, 'liberal' outlook, began to fulfil the hopes and expectations of their guides and guardians. A few colonial students gained access to metropolitan universities almost as of right, on account of their social standing. Instead of considering culture as a gift and a pleasure, the intellectual who emerged therefrom now saw it as a personal distinction and privilege. He might have suffered mild persecution at the hands of the colonialists, but hardly ever really in the flesh. From his wobbly pedestal, he indulged in history and sociology of his country, and thereby managed to preserve some measure of positive involvement with the national processes. It must however be obvious that the degree of national consciousness attained by him was not of such an order as to permit his full grasp of the laws of historical development or the thorough-going nature of the struggle to be waged, if national independence was to be won.

If Ojukwu does not rid himself of this mentally-castrated team of advisers, this Tom-intellectuated harem of political prostitutes, he may soon find himself being identified with them by the masses and before very long discover, to his irremediable woe, that they have all been fighting the same enemy but for far far different reasons. If he does not act now, he might find out sooner than he thinks that 'Biafra' is just another Nigeria in the making, that seeds of disintegration which thrived unseen in the 'homogeneous' newly-independent state of Nigeria is just as prevalent today in the 'homogeneous' newly-seceded state of 'Biafra', that some 'Biafrans' of today could become the 'Calabarians' of tomorrow just as some Nigerians of yesterday have become the 'Biafrans' of today.

The only way to avert this catastrophe is to kill these seeds of social disintegration in 'Biafra' with the insecticide of socialism before they sprout to prove 'Biafra' only a transitory expression of a process of continuous fragmentation which will one day wind up in the 'Democratic Republic of Izuogu'.

Some people might argue that socialism is a good thing but it will be unrealistic for Ojukwu to concern himself with the Hausa and Yoruba masses who may not want his socialism. My immediate reaction to this will be to avoid being as dogmatic as the arguer in presuming to know how the Hausa and Yoruba masses will react since no one has approached them that way before. What I can do, however, is to illustrate what has happened elsewhere under similar circumstances and leave the rest to Ojukwu's strategy of approach and how far he is prepared to cooperate with underground socialist forces already at work on both sides of the Niger, and, since Gowon has betrayed a negotiating trust at Aburi and made a few clumsy attempts to by-pass Ojukwu and negotiate with the 'Biafran' populace, whether Ojukwu does not think it is high time he too cut the grass beneath this man's feet by ignoring him now and negotiating directly with the masses of 'Nigeria' on a more effective and ideologically sophisticated level.

Not long ago, in the late nineteenth and early twentieth century, China was exactly like Nigeria before the current crisis.

China was just a conglomeration of provinces vying, fighting and bickering with each other. Foremost among them was the province of Hunan belonging to the sub-tropical region of Southern China. The Hunanese were, to a startling degree, like the Ibos of Nigeria. The Hunanese were a tough, dynamic and go-getting people. They were great eaters of red-peppers and were noted for their vigorous personalities, and also for their political talents. Mao Tse-tung is a Hunanese. 'China can only be conquered', says a proverb, 'when all the Hunanese are dead.' And in fact during the past century the natives of this province have distinguished themselves in the most diverse causes. Their history glitters with such names as Tseng Kuo-fan, the great scholar whose 'Hunanese Army' crushed the Taipin rebellion, names like T'an Ssu-t'ung, the famed martyr of the 1898 Reform Movement, names like Huang Hsing, the chief military leader of the T'ung Meng Hui. Huang Hsing once described the Hunan province as 'a bomb full of gunpowder ready to blow up, waiting for us to light the fuse'.

Like the Ibos of Nigeria, the Hunanese were hated for their genius and were soon the target of jealousy and victimisation by other provinces. Their land, because of its high mountain ranges, cut through by four major rivers, made it from ancient times a favourite haunt of bandits. Naturally, a time came when the Hunanese felt they had had enough. Hunanese nationalism was soon born and secession was even threatened. But Mao Tse-tung refused. He saw into the future and strongly opposed the growing nationalism of his people. Today, the same Hunanese 'traitor' and the eleven men who stood by him at that time are controlling the eight hundred million people of China.

So much for the 'unrealistic' nature of trying to compromise with the enemies of the Ibos. It is about time the Ibos who, like the Hunanese, are proud of their toughness and rightly so, asked themselves whether it is more compatible with toughness to run away from the field of battle at the first sound of the enemy's canon, or to overcome the initial shock and use the Hunanese magic to mesmerise the enemy into submission.

It is also important that Ojukwu remembers what Professor S. E. Finer said in *The Man on Horseback*, namely that 'practically every successful act of military supplantment has been succeeded by struggle among the victorious conspirators'. I agree with Douglas Rogers when he writes that 'it is time some serious thinking were done in Africa about this situation. It is obvious that, in West Africa at least, professional armies (usually inherited from colonialism) cannot be trusted. Are the people so disillusioned with politicians that they prefer to be ruled by soldiers? If so a new standard of politics is required and when this standard is established, it is better to abolish the professional armies and, for internal security, to set up, as President Sekou Toure has done in Guinea, a People's Militia, giving the workers and farmers the arms whereby they may defend their democratic rights'.

I hope I have not given the impression, especially when I was talking about my articles of 1962, that I claim to be a political philosopher with clairvoyant powers. On the contrary, I am sure there are a good many people to whom some of the points I have belaboured in this essay will seem quite elementary. The answer to the problems of our people is there for anyone to see who cares to look for it. The trouble is that, for too many years, far too many of us have been too busy collecting university degrees to see how futile it is to seek academic and professional security in a country without political stability. I also hope it is clear I have recommended neither secession nor unification, neither weak Federation nor strong Centralisation, neither Hausa domination nor Ibo domination: and I have not advocated any of these not because I have no views of my own or want to remain noncommittal, but for the simple reason that, to me, it is far more important to smash the system which has made us pigs in the eyes of the world, hungry in the midst of plenty and assassins in the tropics of love. It is only when we have decided what system is best suited to our needs that we can decide how best to install the system, whether as one Nigeria, as innumerable seceded 'Biafras' or just a bunch of stateless anarchists running about on the banks of the Niger. Major Nzeogwu was once reported as saying:

If I may borrow your metaphor, the atmosphere is admittedly somewhat cloudy. But I don't think there will be rain. Indeed if you look steadily up you will find that the sun is not yet set and might still peep through. The trouble is that people generally cannot tell which is a rain cloud and which is not, and as a result they tend to be confused. As you know there is too much bitterness at present in the country, and in the past people imagined that they could conveniently do without one another. But the bitterness will clear in the end and they will long be together. Even now the Easterners say they do not want beef from the North, but the same beef comes to them through the West and the Mid-West and even through Duala in the Cameroons, the only difference is that they pay more for it. The same applies to the Northerners. It may take ten or fifteen years for them to come together again but there is no doubt, as far as I can see, that they will. You see, in this world of imperfection, it is sometimes very difficult to capture the ideal. But we can, at least, start with the second best.

No wonder Nzeogwu had to die. With his brilliance of perspective, they had to get him out of the way fast. They shot him in the back and blamed it on the war. And, as always, a Black hand was hired to squeeze the trigger that boomed down on the pages of Black history another Black suicide.

When will my people ever learn? The unbearable thought is that the war that has cost my native land thousands of Black lives is not even our own war. Like every so-called tribal war that erupts in Africa today, it is an imperialist war. The British Government claims to be backing 'Nigeria', while the British businessmen are selling arms secretly to 'Biafra'. De Gaulle claimed to have been aiding Ojukwu, while his personnel were in Lagos getting along famously with Gowon; and, knowing how sensitive the 'Federals' are in these matters, we can hazard a guess what fate would have befallen the Gaullist diplomats in Lagos if their role in the war had been as one-sided as meets the eye. The American record of consistent double game in Black African conflicts and why they play it has already been mentioned elsewhere and need not be repeated again. The International Red Cross is supposed to be sending relief aid to 'Biafra' and, by the weirdest of coincidences, their planes always seem to be ready at hand to be 'seized' whenever the Federal Government run out of planes to carry emergency arms to the front. The trend of the war itself is even more revealing. When the 'Biafrans' captured the Mid-West and threatened to overrun 'Nigeria', sudden massive military aid was bombarded into 'Nigeria' from all sides and the course of the war was successfully averted, with Ojukwu robbed of victory. And when the 'Federals' captured Owerri and threatened to overrun 'Biafra', sudden mysterious military aid was pumped into 'Biafra' from all sides and with enough speed to rob Gowon of victory.

The truth of the matter is that the imperialist does not want any side to have a decisive win in the conflict. Because to do so will put the victorious side in a position of strength to negotiate its economy with the interested powers who have got their claws into the wealth and oil of the country. But as long as there is no clear victory on either side, the West can always blackmail one side with the potential military reaction of the other which only the West, the big imperialist overlord, could forestall. That is why whenever there is stalemate in the war, whenever the victory is going neither one way nor the other, that is when the British Prime Minister picks up his pipe and tobacco and goes scampering off to Lagos to negotiate peace in a hurry.

The interest of the British in Nigeria is not one Nigeria,

but a Nigeria in which they can arbitrate the economy of the country. With the corrupt old politicians poised on the periphery of power in Lagos to take over the country and form another corrupt neo-Tombo Okotiebo-type government, the Establishment is once again trying to dig another Black man's grave in Africa and call it a democratic country.

The Gowons and the Ojukwus will come and go but our dilemma will remain with us as long as our people refuse to learn that the only way to stop these dry-balled Yorkshire Lilliputs sucking our blood is to unite now and sock it to them.

Destroy This Temple

IT IS impossible to outline here a complete catalogue of the motives which compelled me to write a 'murder document'. Let me state at once that it has nothing to do with Enoch Powell as an individual. Nevertheless, I will not go so far as to share the view often expressed by certain Black intellectuals that Powell is 'a good chap, really, because he is not a hypocrite like the rest.' A punk does not cease to be a punk simply because he admits he is a punk. White conservative hopefuls have called Powellism 'White Blacklash', which is equally ridiculous. There has been no forward movement of Whites in England to lash back from. Others have tried to depict it as the White counterpart of Black Power, which is another way of saying that Black Power is 'Powellism in Reverse'. Many people have been fooled by this. I have received countless letters in this prison, both from Whites and Blacks, and most of them have argued that if Enoch Powell is allowed to be free to continue spreading his poisonous propaganda, they see no reason why I should be arrested and locked up behind bars. I must admit I feel flattered by the concern of so many people over my safety and the injustice of my plight. But I find this line of argument most distressing. To place me on the same racialist plane with Powell betrays a lamentable lack of understanding of my angle of involvement.

Mine is a rebellion of the enslaved man against men who make slaves of other men. But Powellism, on the other hand, is the rebellion of the slave-master against the slave. And when a slave-master starts revolting against the slave of his own creation, when a renowned Greek scholar and top politician begins to rave and rant in all seriousness that the Black rubbish-sweepers of British streets should be held responsible for the collapse of an Empire over which the sun never used to set, and that their repatriation to the East from whence they came will make the sun rise from the West, that state racialism is the answer to individual racialism, that the state must discriminate in order that the individual will not discriminate, then the contrast between the stupidity of this 'logic' and the brain of the man stating it is obvious.

I do not believe for one moment that Mr Powell cares one bit whether or not the Black man lives in England in hundreds of millions. I am convinced that Mr Powell is merely fulfilling a function. He is dutifully carrying out a political function allotted to him by the Establishment. And that duty is simply to strengthen the hands of the British Government to abolish the Black Commonwealth status as a prelude to joining the European Common Market. Mr Powell is only a member of a team, playing a role assigned to him to the best of his ability. All the noise, his 'dismissal', and the pious anti-Powell protestations in high places are only part of a well-planned drama to fool, once again, my people and the ever-gullible members of the British public. The prospect of becoming Prime Minister one day might have helped to induce Mr Powell to accept his role of the Hammer of the Blacks, but the real reason behind the eruption and the strategic timing of so-called Powellism is that members of the European Club have decreed the annihilation of the Black Commonwealth status a pre-condition for Britain joining the Market.

Every one of those men at the top knows this for a fact; for has it not been evident that Mr Powell only advocates, while the others implement? And with the same rapidity they condemn him in words. They go to Scarborough to decry Powell publicly as the iniquitous Guru and, while the echo of their jibes is still ringing in the air, they rush off to Gibraltar, pipe in hand, to out-Guru Powell in a Kith-and-kin Tiger talk with 'Rebel Smith', discussing the future of a country with 98 per cent of the population not represented because they were Black.

I have no quarrel with Powell as a man. For I am sure that, to Powell the man, I am as irrelevant as he is to me. Powellism is not a dialogue between Black and White. It is purely a communication between Britain and 'Europe'. Even

at the height of his tirades, Powell, I know, was not talking
to me. He was talking over me, to Europe. Even when he
called us grinning piccaninnies, I was well aware he was
talking about me, but not to me. He was addressing Europe.
De Gaulle, on behalf of the Six, warned Britain long ago to
'do something' about her Commonwealth 'obligations', if
she was serious about joining Europe, not to saddle the Six
with 'it'. Powell is not a man; he is a reply, a manifestation
of the European traditional attitude to my people. To fight
Powell alone is to misplace my enthusiasm and my energy,
to do what they want me to do. No, I refuse to be distracted.

'It has long been the belief of modern men,' writes Du
Bois in *The World and Africa*,

> that the history of Europe covers the essential history of
> civilisation, with unimportant exceptions; that the progress
> of the white race has been along the one natural, normal
> path to the highest possible human culture . . . On the
> other hand, we know that the history of modern Europe
> is very short; scarcely a moment of time as compared with
> that of eternal Egypt. The British Empire is not more
> than two hundred and fifty years old; France in her present
> stature dates back three hundred years; the United States
> was born only a hundred and seventy years ago; and
> Germany less than one hundred years. When, therefore,
> we compare modern Europe with the great empires which
> have died, it is not far different in length of days from
> the empires of Persia, Assyria, the Hittites, and Babylon.
> Ethiopia ruled the world longer than England has. It is
> surely a wider world of infinitely more peoples that Europe
> has ruled; but does this reveal eternal length of rule and
> inherent superiority in European manhood, or merely the
> temporary possession of a miraculously greater brute
> force? Mechanical power, not deep human emotion nor
> creative genius nor ethical concepts of justice, has made
> Europe ruler of the world. Man for man, the modern
> world marks no advance over the ancient; but man for
> gun, hand for electricity, muscle for atomic fission, these
> show what our culture means and how the machine has

conquered and holds modern mankind in thrall. What in our civilisation is distinctly British or American? Nothing. Science was built on Africa and Religion on Asia. Was there no other way for the advance of mankind? Were there no other cultural patterns, ways of action, goals of progress, which might and may lead man to something finer and higher? Africa saw the stars of God; Asia saw the soul of man; Europe saw and sees only man's body, which it feeds and polishes until it is fat, gross, and cruel.

For thirty long years of my life, I lived in a trance. Like countless African students of my generation who were herded into Britain every year to 'receive education', I was living a lie. I was told that Africa was a dark continent and that Europe was the only source of light. I was taught that nothing ever happened in any part of the world till the White man came along. I was made to believe that my people were a mere clay for moulding and my native land only a barren slate where every European had a divine liberty to come and engrave his notions of right and wrong. I was told that my mother was ugly because her skin was black, her hair curly, and her nose and lips unlike the White woman. It was drummed into the plastic mentality of my childhood, that Blackness is incompatible with respectability, and that Black Beauty was only a horse. I went to school five times a week and also to church during the vital part of my developing years to see God and his Angels depicted as White men on Christian posters and the devil himself looking the split image of my dad. I was stripped before the whole school and whipped with boiled chord till I bled every time I committed the 'mortal sin' of joining my people in our traditional juju chant at the Village Assembly Square; and of course had to cleanse myself through Confession, penance and the Holy Communion, before I was allowed into the Sacristy to serve Mass behind the White priest chanting and presiding over the 'holy' ritual of White religion. I was baptised into White Catholicism when I was only four days old and given the name Benedict because I was too young to protest. I learned to live with the cruel dilemma in which the Christian Bible which alone was ordained to offer me salvation had already condemned me from the time of Noah to eternal racial pariahdom through the famous 'Curse of Ham'. I was reared up to accept without question the alleged cultural insignificance of my ancestry and to look upon the European doxy as the only orthodoxy. I was told I was born ignoble and my only hope of atoning for the heinous crime of being African was to dedicate myself to the task of Anglicising myself in European institutions for the rest of my life. I was lied to, right, left and centre, till I couldn't wait to get away from home. And, naturally, at the earliest opportunity, I escaped from the 'jungle' of Africa to the promised Caucasian lustre of England where the White kiss of life would evolve me, under-developed as I am, into a real human being in civilised Europe.

I was to find out later that I had left one jungle for another. I had left 'uncivilised' Africa to come looking for a Shangri-La, only to discover a Powell-infested Babylon in which, in the words of Cecil Roberts in *Wide is the Horizon*, there is more sex and less love, more food and less flavour, more luxury and less comfort, more wealth and less satisfaction, more speeches and less sense, more creeds and less religion than anywhere else in the world. I came groping for explanation and found more intellectuals and less intelligent men, more theory and less practice, more liberals and less freedom, more peace-talks and less peace-programmes, more Marxists and less revolution, more mechanisation and less civilisation, more laws and less justice. To paraphrase Lerone Bennett Jr paraphrasing Leslie Fiedler in *The Negro Mood*, I came to consult the White oracle to demystify my Black abnormality, only to find that my celebrated White fountain of knowledge and normality spends his childhood as imaginary Indian, his adolescence as imaginary Negro, and his adulthood as *imaginary* White. Man, I had come in search of an Eldorado and found a Helldorado.

This realisation was the beginning of self-redemption. But the discovery did not come at once. It took years of painful introspection.

The first painful truth I found out about myself in England was that I was a punk. Like every Black man or woman living in the so-called Mother-country, I had come here to be a beneficiary of the Anglo-Saxon capitalism that thrives on sucking the blood of my people back home in Africa. Some of us have come here to get better jobs and a higher standard of living. Others have come in search of higher 'education' which, in the long run, will give them the same rewards, better jobs and a higher standard of living. But England, a tiny country with nothing much more than coal for its natural resources, is only in a position to offer us these rewards because she loots it off the land of our people. It seems to me contradictory to call England an imperialist monster and, at the same time, be contented to live in England to partake of the fruits of the imperialist monstrosity of England.

I hated to admit this about myself but it was nevertheless the cruel truth. And I realised that to refuse to accept this truth was to apologise for, and even defend, my indirect living off the bloody looting of my people. For a receiver of stolen property, knowing that what he receives is stolen, is as much guilty of the crime of theft as the man who did the actual stealing; and even more so if the victims of the robbery are one's defenceless little brothers and sisters who have been rendered even more defenceless because one has run away from home, deserting home at the hour of need when nothing short of united defence could fend off the invader. I realised that unless I faced this ugly truth about my present treacherous historical role, I would never develop the moral courage to give me the revolutionary aptitude to change that role, that unless I came to terms with myself, I should have spent my childhood in Africa being an imaginary savage, my adolescence in England being an imaginary White man, and my post-college adulthood being a real savage. In short, I had come to England to feed fat on the fruits stolen from my father and nurtured with the manure of my mother's flesh.

It is true I did not come to England of my own choice. It is true that if the Chinese had colonised my country I should be in China today, not England. It is true I am only a tiny speck in the wind of history and that I come here, not because I enjoy slotting shillings for heat, but because the uninvited White man came to my native land first and created a one-sided economic wind that is still blowing me and my Black brothers to his shores. It is true that the Englishman is the last person to ask me what right I have to be here because he ought to know from his own history that he too is an immigrant here, that his claim to England is having enjoyed the usufruct possession of this island as a second-hand German immigrant, and that he therefore has no claim as an immigrant to arrogate to himself the right to demand of another immigrant, Black or non-Black, the right to come here and the power to regulate his numbers. It is true that all this is true, that it is an unchallengeable fact that I am not here of my choice but simply a victim of an unfortunate historical current that has carried me while still asleep from the shores of the have-nots to the land of the haves to make me a have at the expense of my people.

But is it not equally true that when a man is asleep in a boat by the sea-shore and wakes up suddenly to find himself in the middle of the ocean where the wind has blown him with the current against his will, is it not equally true that he must fight hard to steer his boat back to his shores? Does a drowning man who finds that his boat has been capsised contrary to his will not fight the waves desperately to swim home to safety? These were the questions that tormented me night and day in those early days of realisation.

But even in the middle of this resolve, I was very aware that older generations than mine have gone back to Africa after studying in England and, far from redeeming our people, have tightened the chains on their ankles. It becomes obvious that a physical return to Africa is meaningless unless it is preceded by a psychological return. This emphasises the fact that something is desperately wrong with the 'education' we come to 'receive' in Europe. Some of us have claimed, in a way of apologising for our attachment to Europe, that we have come over here to balance the economic and political equation which the White man has kept one-sided ever since the Portuguese set foot on Congo soil in 1495. But are we really balancing that equation? Or are we not indeed widening the gap of that economic imbalance by voluntarily remaining exposed to an 'education' designed by a man who wants to keep us perennially subordinate?

What power, pride and self-confidence can we, as Black people, hope to derive from a system of education in which, to use the words of Du Bois in *The World and Africa*, White 'National heroes were created by lopping off their sins and canonising their virtues, so that Gladstone had no connection with slavery, Chinese Gordon did not get drunk, William Pitt was a great patriot and not an international thief. Education was so arranged that the young learned not necessarily the truth, but that aspect and interpretation of the truth which the rulers of the world wished them to know and to follow.'

Since I could not obviously find the answer in European books, I turned to works created by the older generation of African writers themselves. I consulted the celebrated Heinemann's Library of 'African Educational' publications and its equivalents, in the hope that the award-winning Western-famed African novelists, dramatists, essayists and artists would put the African personality in focus for me.

My discoveries can best be summarised by a paragraph which appeared in Robert F. Williams' *Crusader* written— it is interesting to note—from his own independent observation:

It must be borne in mind that a great portion of material produced by black intellectuals under the aegis of the white power structure is anti-black and pro-white. White publishers are the most forceful advocates of Americanism. With but a few exceptions they have seen to it that black works of art and literature comply with the white concept of the 'nigra's place in American life'. The white man's power to publish or not publish has deprived the black artist of the right to reflect black truth as it relates to savage America. Because of the racist white man's life and death control over the black man's art, it has become a vehicle of accomodation, steeped in racist clichés that surreptitiously debase our people and serve the cause of white supremacy.

Too often, as a price of publication, the racist power structure has required the black artist to reduce himself and the entire race to a state of immoral clowns and idiots. The cunning racist white man, in a subtle effort to put the black man down through his own works, requires the 'award winning' Afro-American novel, autobiography, cinema or theatrical production to be self-deriding exercises in negro crime, vulgarity, prostitution, dope addiction, homosexuality, incest, self-hate and psychopathic masochism.

A close examination of much of this work will reveal a thinly veiled attack on the integrity and intelligence of the race. It is not protest but the condemnation of black by black. The most tragic aspect of this whole affair is the fact that nigra intellectuals are inclined to judge the merit of their own art and literature on the basis of the white man's reviews, publicity or hypocritical glorification. If the black art is going to disembowel the race before the entire world, what greater instrument of justification does the enemy oppressor need to convince the world that he is truly the Christian benefactor and civilizer of the 'savage African?' Why should the racist devil object to a transfer of the means of black degradation to a different but more effective crew of white supremacy?

Though written with the black writer in America specifically in mind, it struck me that the home-truth of Robert F. Williams' analysis is even truer about the academic-titled literary Sambo-darlings of the West in Africa, with of course the exception of a core of a few courageous young 'extremists', 'racists' and 'too-political no-goods' who will, they hope, pass away unpublished, unknown, ostracised, rejected from script to script, dead and unremembered victims of the white Kingmaker's freeze.

It became apparent to me from then onwards that one must begin with the rejection of the definitions of the West. Power

is the ability to define. I must put an end to letting the
White man define me to myself. I must kill once and for all
the five hundred-years-old induced complex whereby my life
has been controlled by the whims of the White imperialist.
It is ridiculous to continue to accept Western definitions
without question when I am in the sorry state I am today
because the West has defined me as such. What I ought to
do is, psychologically for a start, render the West irrelevant
to my being. I am, therefore I am.

The emasculation of the Black man dated from the day he
empowered a hungry buccaneer outsider to define blackness.
The Black man became a Negro the day he was baptised
by a preacher whose God was white and devil black. The
Negro was the invention of a greedy speculator who invested
millions of pounds on the self-hate and gullibility of Blacks.
The African became 'the native' the day he called a stranger
who arrived with an empty suitcase from Europe 'Bwana'.
Africa became the 'dark continent' the moment the African
accepted the insulting equation that Black = Evil + Savagery
+ Shame. And Europe became the Black Man's Burden the
day they christened the Third World the 'White Man's
Burden'.

The writing and interpretation of history must be done
by those who genuinely aim to explain the past to elucidate
the present, and never again by intellectual crooks hired by
empire-builders to distort and efface their ugly past in order
to justify their even uglier present. The ambition of every
invader is to keep control of the territory he has captured.
Everything he does, no matter how humane it seems on the
surface, has this objective in view. His programme of aid
and education, his divine mission of introducing the captive
populace to a God godlier than theirs, his new laws, new
politics, fine culture, and fine civilising benevolence, will
soon prove, on the day of reckoning, to be no more and no
less than a mere excuse and systematic plan to extend his
stay and consequent extraction of booty. This is the story of
my homeland in Africa.

The White man told us on arrival that we suffer from
leprosy. True. That we exude malaria. Granted. But he

conveniently forgot to mention that he suffers from maladies and neuroses our people have not even today heard about. He declared instead that we Africans have a monopoly of the diseases of the body. Beautiful. He never told us though that the viruses of the mind which plague his society back home in Europe are far more destructive of human personality than any bodily disease we knew before he came. He was eager to teach us that our infant mortality is astronomically high. But it eluded him that his suicide mortality is astronomically higher. In effect, what he was asking us to do was to get rid of one mortality and replace it with another.

The acceptance of this formula for national decay was the beginning of the woe of my people.

To support his view of the world, the White 'civiliser' dished out facts upon facts from his books to persuade my people.

And the unfortunate thing about it is that Fact, by definition, is not the whole truth. Fact is only an absence of contradiction. As such, it does not guarantee the whole truth. For example, if my landing officer in this prison were to ask me tomorrow morning what I was doing at this time of the night and I reply simply that I was writing a letter, I have stated a fact. It is a fact as indisputable as the existence of Brixton Prison itself. My landing officer might even pat me on the back for doing something as harmless as writing a letter. He might even extend my light-out time tomorrow night since I employ my time so usefully and innocuously, based on the indisputable fact that I am writing a letter. But what this fact does not reveal to him is that, knowing that a letter like this would never pass the censors, I am in fact writing it on stolen toilet rolls of paper soon to be smuggled out of this prison, contrary to regulation. In effect, I shall have told him a fact which has indeed concealed the truth.

What I am driving at is that facts can be used for two contradicting purposes: to impart information, and to conceal information. A few nights ago, the prison chaplain asked me if I found the copy of the Bible in my cell useful. I nodded enthusiastically and told him that I did indeed use it every single night. I went so far as to tell him that I could not go to sleep happily and peacefully without it. What I said to him was a fact of course. I cannot go to sleep peacefully without the Bible because all I do with it is put it under the bed-rug to use it as a pillow at night.

This proves that facts are not as reliable in assessing situations as we often suppose. There is nothing more dangerous than facts in the hands of the imperialist devil out to quote scriptures for his purpose. Hitler used facts to justify the murder of six million Jews. Lynch mobs in the United States of America used facts to justify the lynching and roasting alive of 3,397 black men and women between 1882 and 1938 alone. Capitalist economists use facts to destroy, even today, tons of edible food while two human beings out of every three in the world are dying of starvation. They used facts also to prove to me and my people that we had no culture, no history, no civilisation. And we believed them. For countless years of my life, they have used facts to keep me living in a trance.

One day, I asked them to tell me why Britain was called Great. They boasted of an empire which was reclaimed from the sea of the blood of my people. I asked them why Britain was called Christian. They pointed out the epitome of British Christianity, St Paul's Cathedral of course, which is festooned with the monuments, shields and swords of generals who acquired their saintly pinnacles by the number of men they beheaded. I asked them why Britain was called philanthropic and, having got wiser, they side-stepped Cecil Rhodes and pointed at Enoch Powell and the offer of two thousand pounds he has made us to keep our distance. I asked them for the evidence of their civilisation. They gleefully pointed at the motor cars which, since they are producing more cars than roads to take them, will soon become illegal to drive freely on public streets, having already become illegal to park freely on the streets. They showed me factories roaring with the production of weapons of war. And, to bring me up to date, they indicated on the sky-line of London their sky-scraper Post Office Tower where grown-ups achieve the exciting and incredible feat of eating and moving in circles at the same time. This, to the sky-scraping wise men of the

West, is the acme of human happiness and civilisation. It is also where I split.

Suddenly, I saw it all clearly. I was still frustrated but I was no longer blind. I knew I had to stop kidding myself in White colleges. My tour of America and my meeting with really 'aware' Black people in the ghettoes over there, as opposed to the affected but ineffective, Tom-intellectuated and cowardly, I-am-alright-Old-Boy and Oxford-accented-hustler-type Black 'Englishmen' one was then saddled with in Britain, gave me real hope. I came back to London fully convinced that the road to Black freedom did not lie through Oxford, Cambridge, or the London School of Economics. I realised, even then, that it was a thorny road which might one day run through Brixton Jail and beyond. There was no other way. All other alternative avenues led inevitably to Tranceville. And I was sick and tired of living in a trance, of living a lie, of living a death camouflaged as life.

But a realistic political organisation of Black peoples in England seemed a wild dream. For the Black man in Britain was a victim of two things.

Firstly, he was a victim of self-deception. He had come to the 'Mother Country' to be a beneficiary of Anglo-Saxon capitalism, hoping in all good faith that through his own personal success he might 'exploit' back for his people at home what colonial England had exploited from his people. And there his logic ended and it might have been a fine logic had it not been that neo-colonialism had superseded colonialism, and that the rate at which he was 'exploiting' England was laughably minute in comparison with the rate the neo-colonialist West was looting our home country. The Black man in England thus occupies a unique position. He is an ambivalent being, the only ghetto bourgeois in the world. Even though he largely sweeps the streets of England, he occupies, in relation to his people back home, a curious position compatible to a relationship between the bourgeoisie and the proletariat. He sees himself, worker or student, as being 'better off' and, with a little encouragement from White 'Troubadour liberals' and permissively inclined flesh-crazy White girl friends, he genuinely sees Britain as a heaven and considers himself the luckiest and most privileged Black man in the whole wide world. The Black man in England, by definition therefore, is a Tom, with one eye on the House of Lords, if he is an 'intellectual' or a cricketer, and the other eye on the Lordship of some Lambeth property, if he is a 'ghetto bourgeois'. Anyone who was a Black political activist in Britain in the days when I returned from America knows how difficult it was to approach a man like that and even suggest that Britain, a White country that actually offered him his fat money packet every Friday, a house and White wife into the bargain, was exploiting him. He would call you mad, accuse you of 'talking stupidness, man,' and if you were reckless enough to ask him to join you in a political Black organisation aimed to destroy the White system that gave him so much, he could kill you on the spot. I need not add here that I have learned this lesson to my cost since the reader is already aware that the printer who handed over my document to the police and who, apart from being responsible for my being in this prison right now, will also be the police key witness at the Old Bailey, is a Black man. More than that, he is my countryman and, if I remember correctly, my very last correspondence with him was the post-card greeting I sent him and his wife from Conakry. I was arrested a few days after I returned from that trip. Illusion is never the best friend of a revolutionary. And one illusion I have learned to do without is that Whites have a monopoly of indolent men.

Secondly, the Black man in Britain is a victim of what I consider the biggest and most publicised myth in the world. It is generally believed that there is very little racialism in Britain. The English have succeeded in fooling the entire world that they are the least racist and most tolerant beings in the world. And whenever a race rebellion occurs in America, the British politicians and journalists are always the first to address the world on TV or in newspapers from thrones of racial innocuousness on how 'this could never happen in this country' because England has very little racial problem and, at any rate, not as much as America. As any intelligent Black man and any honest White man in the country knows, this is the wierdest myth of this century.

I agree there is a difference between the racialism in America and the racialism in England. But I disagree when the Englishman tells me that it is worse in the States. I have been to both countries and studied and experienced the White man's attitudes toward me as a Black man. And I can state without equivocation that racialism in England is far worse.

I will explain myself. To compare the racialism in America with the racialism in England is like comparing a bad slave-master with a good slave-master. I prefer the bad slave-master any day. The bad slave-master at least makes the slave aware that slavery is evil. From his attitude, he can make the slave realise without being coerced that slavery is a wicked thing which must be destroyed at all costs. But the good slave-master is the sly one. He makes the slave think that slavery can be a good thing, that evil can be made palatable, that one can compromise with man's inhumanity to man. The product of good slave treatment is the Uncle Tom. His counterpart in the wicked household is the angry freedom-loving and uncompromising revolutionary.

America is like a wicked slave-master. England is comparable to a 'good' slave-master. In Mississippi, the White man tells you straight that he does not want you in his neighbourhood and you know where you stand with him. In Wimbledon, the Englishman will apologise most profusely when he refuses you accommodation on racial grounds: 'Room to let, sorry no coloureds, Irish or dogs.' When you confront him personally, it is never his fault, he of course never has racial prejudice, it is always the neighbour who is the villain. The American will lynch you and doesn't give a damn who knows it. But the Englishman always has enough residue of subtlety to lynch you with iron hands in velvet gloves. Challenge him with the murder he has just perpetrated and he politely points out to you with the tip of his rolled umbrella that there are no fingerprints on the victim of his 'gentlemanly' brutality to prove his guilt. This is how they have fooled the Black man in England to believe that there is little or no evidence of racialism in the Englishman.

This is the centuries-old method they have employed to make the unsuspecting Black Tom here actually enjoy his slavery. Is it any wonder that at a time when America was producing the fiery Malcolms, Karengas, Carmichaels, Rap Browns and the very concept of Black Power itself, Britain was still churning out Black Sambos to whom going to the House of Lords and having tea with the Queen was the vogue? Isn't it a marvel that, even in the field of art, while the 'ever so horrible' America could boast of her Leroi Jones, Jimmy Baldwin, Lerone Bennett, Sidney Poitier, Cleaver, Sammy Davis Jr, Nina Simone, and countless czars of jazz, our tolerant England, though still boasting of her kinder patronage of Blacks, cannot produce a single Black name to match up with the Black brothers in the States? England has succeeded so well in freezing out her Black talents that the very concept of a Black producer of above Tower Theatre scope is a joke. Songs that owe their origin to unknown Black back-street night clubs in the ghettoes of England have frequently appeared in the top ten under the names of soul-less White 'stars'.

Yet we Black men in England would be the first to tell you that we are happy. To prove this happiness to ourselves we go to the Q Club every night of the week to dance till the early hours of dawn. I have been there myself. It was always a staggering experience to arrive at the Q Club at midnight, to see the miracle. A crowd of what must verge on thousands would crowd into one hall, belly to belly, dancing wildly to the most-deafening system soul beats you ever heard. The noise, the shrieking, the sheer compact of teeming humanity, enough to make you dizzy, in that dimly lit place in the basement, so jammed that you couldn't even force your way through jostles of sweaty and swaying and jumping Black bodies, never failed to fill me with awe. Never in my life had I seen so many Black people in one place. Some go there just for the experience of it. And you always marvelled that there were so many Black youth in this country.

But the most astounding part of it was that the only thing that got us all there together was the music. Nothing else could have done it. Nothing else could do it. Only music and dancing. And we danced and we danced and we danced. But we all danced till nothing else mattered, till all the sorrows in the world dissolved in the mist of our perspiration. Still we danced. We shook our heads, gyrated our hips, tears running down our eyes, while the girls, mini-skirted and nearly topless, danced in a frenzy till their nipples flicked out and their undies tore like sacks. We danced. We were like people in a trance. Which we were.

We had become Zorbas without realising it. Like Zorba the Greek, we were dancing when we should be crying. Like Zorba the dreamer, we were signing our death warrant with the soles of our feet. At the funeral of his only son, Dimitri, Zorba had danced away while everybody else was crying. Asked why he danced, he said that it was the only thing that stopped the pain he felt in his soul. The test of every philosophy lies in the kind of man it produces. What sort of man is Zorba the Greek? He is a failure. He dreams lofty dreams which never ever materialise. He has gigantic ambitions which die stillborn. He watches every dream in his life turn into a nightmare. He has a Midas complex in reverse, with everything he touches turning to clay and crumbling to dust. He leaves destruction wherever he goes and ruins every man who takes him into his confidence, including the woman he marries, let alone himself. Zorba is a tragedy dancing on two legs, and he fails because he abuses pain.

The moral lesson to draw from Zorba's life relevant to me is that pain cannot be sublimated through dancing and laughter. And no man attempts it without caving in. You cannot eliminate human tragedy by pumping laughing gas into the catastrophies of a long-suffering people. As I have said more than once, the primary function of pain, in a normal man, is to give the sufferer the hardihood to isolate himself psychologically from the men who cause him torture and fight them till he frees himself from them physically.

You cannot fight your tormentor with your feet. The shrewd White monopolists know this. That is why they grant the Black man the monopoly of 'soul'. That is why 'soul' has become a thriving Black concern and the one

security from the system of society. On the other hand, the Black man in the ghetto enjoys no such security from the system and that is why he is out to mow down that system through Black Power. Even in the absence of any other considerations, this point at one stroke invalidates White membership of the Black Power movement, and in fact betrays the abject naïvety and the organisational immaturity of even considering it. There is no political revolutionary philosophy, from Karl Marx to any philosophical treatise one cares to mention, in which the secure and the insecure within the same system join hands together to fight to destroy that system.

Yet the White 'Marxists,' with their usual presumption that only they have read Marx, persist in deriding Black Power as narrow, nationalistic, and un-Marxian. One can of course see and understand that the mentality behind this is, perhaps inevitably, the same old supremacist psychology of the White man that the Black man cannot do anything on his own. Even though the White worker has gone Powellist, anti-Black, pro-establishment, reactionary and conservative, the so-called White marxists expect me to wait arm-folded like a good boy until the White worker in the industrial West stops killing me in Vietnam and decides to lead me, in accordance with the decree of Marx, to make world revolution. Meanwhile, I must turn the other cheek when a fascist White worker in a police uniform boots me in the teeth and arrests me for 'assaulting a police officer.'

To the White marxists, it is inconceivable that the Black man could be the vanguard of international revolution and thereby succeed where they had failed.

According to Engels in his Dialectics of Nature, 'All nature, from the smallest thing to the biggest, from a grain of sand to the sun, from the protista to man, is in a constant state of coming into being and going out of being, in a constant flux, in a ceaseless state of movement and change.' In other words, according to Dialectical Materialism, everything in nature and social life undergoes a constant change. Yet when it comes to the historical role of the White working class in industrialised Europe to lead the world revolution, the law of dialectics, according to our White 'marxist' friends, gives up its sacredness and becomes a respecter of White skin, making everything stand still. The fact that the Black man today has become the most oppressed class all over the world and therefore constitutes a new proletariat of his own much more qualified and actively more inclined to lead world revolution, is quite immaterial. It would seem, as Harold Cruse states in *Marxism and the Negro*, that 'thus, the 'White man's burden' shifts from the capitalist's missionaries to the socialist's revolutionaries whose duty to history is to lift the 'backward' peoples from their ignominious state to socialist civilisation even if the Whites have to postpone this elevation abroad until they have managed to achieve it at home. But in doing so, the White Marxist's dialectical conceptions of world developments become a distorted image of the reality that is taking place before their very eyes.' Our White marxist friends must indeed make up their minds whether their Materialism is dialectical or mechanistic.

This is by no means the view of all Black Power organisations. There are those who are of the opinion that, because the White youth of today are beginning to reject their White heroes, the time has come when the Black man must join hands in a world-wide revolution with White radicals, or White liberals as they used to be called. It all sounds very inspiring but experience whispers to me: Beware! The radical White youth has a curious way of cutting his hair when he leaves college and joins the Establishment. Considering that the men who built the British Empire were often men who were radical enough in their youth to leave home and school in disgust to go adventuring into the 'wilds' of the world, I find it hard to accept that the radicalism of youth is a new phenomenon in capitalist Europe. Besides, I don't see how we in the Black Power movement can seriously condemn Martin Luther King for joining hands with Whites and singing 'We shall overcome' if we are prepared to do the same thing in our time. The only difference is that King called them brothers in Christ and we call them radicals today. We may argue that King's White friends were not radical enough for our liking but we cannot deny that, just as our White 'comrades' today are radical enough for us in our own estimation, King's White comrades too were radical enough for him in his own judgement. They were radical Christians. And before we start debating that the two movements are ideologically incompatible, we must be careful not to forget from whose faith Marx borrowed the morality of his revolution. Unless we are prepared to embrace these realities, even if it meant a revision of our programme, we may find ourselves dishonestly indulging in double standards, one for King and another for ourselves.

We must not forget that it was not till Black Power came along and began to organise Black people on a basis of colour that Black revolt began to yield concrete results on an international level. Black civil rights movements failed basically because they ignored the structural realities of the world in which they lived. It would be catastrophic to repeat that mistake by making a dramatic about-turn after we have come this far. A people oppressed all over the world because they are Black cannot ignore this fact when they rally to fight their oppressors.

It is true that Marx called on the workers of the world to unite; but it is equally true that he stated that his philosophy must be applied according to the specific circumstances of the situation. It seems to me the 'followers' of Marx are putting the poor chap in a most awkward position. As is often the fate of Bibles, it would seem that Marx is least understood by those who profess to be his apostolic interpreters. I cannot see how any man who called on workers to unite because they are oppressed as workers could deny men of colour the right to unite when they are victimised as men of colour. I fail to understand how Marx, who has stated unequivocally that 'Labour cannot emancipate itself in the white skin where in the black it is branded,' could have instructed his 'orthodox' followers to raise revolutionary protests when branded-black labour wants to emancipate itself.

I accept that it is a fact of capitalism that the White worker and the Black worker both suffer exploitation. But isn't there another category that overrides this fact? Is it not a fact also that the Black worker is oppressed for two reasons, (a) because he is a Black man and (b) because he is a worker? But the White worker is not oppressed because he is a White man. In other words, a White worker can win the pools any day and, like the White student radical who cuts his hair, decide to join the establishment and escape oppression. But no Black man, no matter how rich he becomes or how long is his festoon of university degrees, can escape being a victim of racial discrimination.

In view of these facts, how can any serious analyst of the Black situation, who does not wilfully blind himself to the economics of racism today, still insist on lumping the Black and White workers under one revolutionary category as sufferers of the same degree of pain? If we accept they are not, why pretend that they are? And why base our Alliance Programme on a distortion of social reality?

I do not deny that good White people exist. On the contrary, I can testify to the existence of many from personal experience. Without attempting to sound cynical, I have many White friends. I have enjoyed my own quota of White friendships in various parts of the world. But, as far as I am concerned, a friend is only a friend, be he Black or White, because we basically regard each other as equals. And if a man genuinely regards me as his equal, he does not think me incapable of solving my own problems. He does not want to do my thinking for me any more than I want to do his for him.

I respect my White friends because they do not tell me to ignore my problem just because they are good White exceptions to the rule. They do not expect me to ignore my problem and concentrate on the exceptions. Anyone who tells me to do that cannot conceivably consider me an adult. Because no thinking adult would have a problem and ignore that problem to concentrate on exceptions to it. And no man who denies me my adulthood on a basis of colour can deny me the right to dismiss him as racist. I therefore reserve the right to discount his friendship because racists don't feature popularly in my circle.

The White people I call friends are the first to recognise

that I have a tough dilemma before me and, because they respect my manhood, expect me to ignore distracting exceptions and get on with the job. This is what those who dismiss my fight against the White man as racist overgeneralisation fail to understand. It is comparable to a situation where my house is on fire. My kitchen is on fire. My lounge is also on fire. But my bedroom is not on fire. Not yet. What they are asking me to do is not to raise a fire alarm because there is an exception in my bedroom. It sounds laughable but this is precisely the level of logic our White-exceptionist pacifists are condemning me for not employing.

Having no Black tradition of racism to draw inspiration from, we founded our Black Power thinking in Britain, not on the hatred of White individuals, but on concrete facts yielded to us by our study and analysis of the relationship between British society and our people. In spite of the illusions being rammed into our people in Britain, the fact remains that we are far from free. They tell us that the British Black man is the freest Black man in the world because he is free to go to Speakers' Corner in Hyde Park and shout as much as he wants. Freedom of speech, they say, represents the quintessence of liberty. Fantastic!

Right here in Brixton Prison, we prisoners are at liberty to scream for freedom and bang our heads on the stone wall of our cells till we bleed to death. We have freedom of speech all right. We have the freedom of shouting and yelling. And many have indeed yelled themselves insane, and wind up in the B Wing, the sepulchre for breathing dead men.

We have become very suspicious of Hyde Park freedom. For the men who exercise free speech in Hyde Park are the most unfree of men. It goes without saying that if they indeed had freedom, there would be no need then for them to howl for it in Hyde Park in the first place. The free speech which the Black man exercises in Hyde Park is a palliative, a state-designed blindfold to stop an unfree man seeing his unfreedom. Free speech is only the vocal 'freedom' to complain, like a shouting prisoner in a cell, about the actual unfreedoms in the land. It does not mean you are free.

When a little boy wants to go and play in the fields, he

is not enjoying this freedom because he is locked up in his room by cruel parents and told he is free to cry at the top of his voice about his unfulfilled desire. The unfreedom is even more cruel when that boy is allowed to look through the window at the distant playgrounds to see what he is missing. The little boy can only attain the real freedom he desires when the door is unlocked and he is able physically to go and play in the fields. Given the choice between shouting for freedom in a locked room and exercising this freedom practically on the playground without being allowed to shout, it is clear that an intelligent boy would rather play in the fields and keep his mouth shut because there would be nothing to shout for now that his wish is granted. A hungry man would rather have his food and tell you what you could do with your verbal freedom to shout for it on an empty stomach.

Yet the Black political thinker cannot open his mouth in England without having freedom of speech being thrust down his throat in place of his demand for freedom for his people.

We never tire of being told that the 'dole' is the Black man's manna from heaven, that the national assistance on which of course every Black man lives in Britain, is the indisputable final proof of the benevolence of democratic freedom. But experience has shown that, just as religion was the spiritual opium of the people, the 'dole' has become the material opium of oppressed humanity today. The greatest insurance against revolution is the 'dole' because there can never be a revolution as long as there are no men hungry to sufficient point of desperation to start it. The same goes for the celebrated National Health 'free' medical aid, which by the way is not free. If a worker is indisposed and cannot afford, or refuses to pay for medical treatment, he stays in his bed at home. This affects productivity in the industry and the man who suffers is the capitalist who cannot deliver his goods in time to bank his profit. So the shrewd capitalist makes sure that his workers have instant medical care when they are ill by making them pay for it in advance. That is all the National Health of Britain means. It is the same shrewd old capitalist fox providing advance lubrication for the human parts of his industrial machine and making them think it is free. The 'dole' and the National Health, far from being, as we are told, symbols of workers' triumph over the big boss, are in reality the greatest capitalist blow to the working man of this country. You can imagine how much more heavily that blow descends on me, the poor Black man who is considered second-class working class.

Because the blow of unfreedom falls heaviest on me, I must make doubly sure that I understand what I demand.

Freedom, as we see it in Black Power thinking, can be defined as man's practical ability to satisfy the basic needs of his being. These needs come under two categories; because every man has two fundamental urges which impel his every action in life.

The first is what I call the Primary Urge. It is the basic desire in man to satisfy the needs of his body with regard to food, clothing, shelter and equality of opportunity of access to the amenities of his social environment such as education. It becomes striking immediately that the main characteristic of this Primary Urge is that it makes man want to *take* from his environment.

What I call the Secondary Urge, or the Ultimate Urge in man, we can define as the urge which every man feels to fulfil himself through creative work. Contrary to the Primary Urge, the significant thing about the Secondary Urge is that it makes man want to *give* to his environment. Just as the Primary Urge makes a man hungry to take in, the Secondary Urge makes him hungry to give out of his being. Everybody has a 'talent' for something. Some have it for writing poetry, some for reading it movingly, some for farming, some for carpentry, some for singing opera, some for tapping palm-wine, every human being has a 'talent' to create something, and the urge which impels him inside to give expression to and translate into external reality this burning creative potentiality within his soul we call the Secondary Urge. It is only through its expression that ultimate self-fulfilment is attained.

As the name suggests, the Secondary Urge is indeed

secondary to the Primary Urge but in the final analysis much more important. It is secondary because the human body must be fed, clothed, sheltered and kept alive, which is the department of the Primary Urge, before spiritual self-fulfilment is feasible through response to the Secondary Urge. It is more important because it is only through spiritual self-fulfilment that true happiness in life is achieved.

The inability of Western man to understand this dialectical equilibrium between the two urges in man is the bane and bore of Western philosophy. At one time, Western philosophers lay all the emphasis on the Secondary Urge and call themselves idealists. The succeeding generation will lay all their emphasis on the Primary Urge and call themselves materialists. The result is that Western philosophers have been repeating themselves over and over again for centuries. The philosophy of the West has become recurrent, and every succeeding generation, while pretending to be saying something new, indulges in the compilation of a new dictionary of sentences designed to clothe threadbare old ideas in new phraseologies. And they succeed so well that they even deceive themselves.

The organisation of the Western economies is also such that it tends to be anti-human fulfilment because it frustrates the Primary Urge in the majority and stifles the Secondary Urge in all. I do not propose to speak for the militant students and the communists, but I believe this is a fair summary of their grievance. Theirs is a healthy opposition when it is genuine and deserves to be encouraged.

Man in society is forced to spend his whole life striving to cater for his body and, the harder he plods, the more that body is exploited and the greater his needs become. From cradle to grave, that man fights incessantly but in vain to nurse his Primary Urge. His Secondary Urge is ignored and, with the passing of years, becomes ultimately repressed. Deprived of the true happiness which comes only through creative self-fulfilment, he loses the capacity for real happiness and the appetite for it into the bargain. He falls out of love with life, loses the ability to laugh, and whenever he reads of a happier period in past history or meets 'natives' from communal or semi-communal cultures of the world, his only explanation for their happiness, laughter and general love of life is that they are immature. But, when the chips are down, the plain truth is that, being a product of a frustrated Primary Urge with a brutally stunted Secondary Urge, the Western cynic is an incomplete man, unfulfilled, under-developed, in short a bowler-hatted savage. Happily there are some who have fought this condition and come out on top to join the human race. The less able remain a prey of the unfreedom which masquerades as freedom. Whether they do not see it because they cannot see it or cannot see it because they will not see it is no concern of mine any more. I may be speaking of Europe to demonstrate the brutal techniques of European colonialism and what eunuchs it has made of me and my people. I have quit speaking to Europe. I cast no blame and waste no recommendations on Europe. I have a more pressing job to do.

I can hear the call of Frantz Fanon in *The Wretched of the Earth*. 'My brothers,' he cries, 'how is it that we do not understand that we have better things to do than to follow that same Europe? That same Europe where they were never done talking of Man, and where they never stopped proclaiming that they were only anxious for the welfare of Man: today we know with what sufferings humanity has paid for every one of their triumphs of mind. Come then, comrades, the European game has finally ended; we must find something different.'

For us, that something different is what we call Black Power today. Black Power is not something I am imposing on anyone. It is not like colonialism where, as Jean-Paul Sartre aptly explained in the Preface to *The Wretched of the Earth*, 'there must be intimidation and thus oppression grows. Our soldiers overseas, rejecting the universalism of the mother country, apply the 'numerous clauses' to the human race: since none may enslave, rob or kill his fellow-man without committing a crime, they lay down the principle that the native is not one of our fellow-men. Our striking-power has been given the mission of changing this abstract certainty into reality: the order is given to reduce the inhabitants of the annexed country to the level of superior monkeys in order to justify the settler's treatment of them as beasts of burden.'

I do not intend to annex England to Africa. I do not think I need her coal that desperately in the tropics. I have no ambition to reduce the inhabitants of England to the level of superior monkeys. Not even the swastika-bearers. I think they have been able to do quite well for themselves in this direction. No, it is not part of my programme to impose Black Power ideals on the White man, or make him speak my language, or put on my African traditional dress or gobble the Black man's culture. Black Power simply means that I want to be me and that people must no longer stand between me and myself. I want to stop living a lie. I am not a White man and see no reason why I should pretend to be one. As I write this very moment, I am thinking in my African language and translating very fast into English. And all because White Power saw in my native Blackness a mere vacuum to extend its domain. Black Power means that all this ridiculous irregularity must stop. It means that I must not have a foreign tongue artificially inseminated into my mouth. It means that I must begin to see and react to life itself from my own Black experience. And on a more personal level, it means that African literature must begin to be realistic, even if it means being 'pessimistic'.

We do not dream for one moment that the Black people in Britain can organise themselves as a unit totally separate from other Black forces in the world. Black Power is an international concept. How each local group enforces its philosophy depends on the local social specifics. The Black man in South Africa can hardly be expected to employ the same tactics as the Black man in Hungary. The British Black man, being the Jonah in the belly of the shark, has a tremendous brunt to bear. He has not come here of his choice but the fact is he is here. And as long as he is here, he must defend himself.

While it is not our policy to impose Blackness on the White man, it is our more immediate policy not to let anyone come between us and our Blackness, be he civilian, soldier, or police. We know that the indifferent Englishman is an accomplice of imperialism. And since he too is, perhaps in more decadent ways, a victim of the same imperialism, we are tolerant enough to let him be and die his own slow death. But those police officers who use unprovoked violence in the oppression of my people must not grumble when we devise tactics to defend ourselves. When a custodian of the law who is supposed to defend me, the helpless minority, turns round to be my tormentor himself and uses his uniform as a cover for the swastika medallion on his chest, no Black wife and child can call a Black father a man who does not defend them from such a uniformed coward.

And here I must stop. To talk about police brutality to the Black people in Britain is to preach to the converted, in fact to be a bore. One thing that all the Black organisations in Britain agree about, even movements as ideologically wide apart as CARD and the Black Power Movement, is that the Black man has been taxed to the limit of his patience by increasing police brutality. Black ghettoes are deluged with leaflets all over the country and to repeat what the Black people are saying in those leaflets about police treatment of Black people would be to make this book unprintable.

I have been called a monster for being the author of the document which the police have described as a plot to murder them. Anyone who has read every word in this book and remembers the incidents which led up to the writing of that document and yet calls me a monster is perfectly entitled to his opinion. But he would do well to remember that, behind the Black monster, there is a White Frankenstein.

As for how this Black monster feels behind bars right now in Brixton Prison, I must turn to Dostoyevsky, that other monster who was so monstrous that he once faced a firing squad, to borrow words adequate enough to describe my spirit in this cruel heart of Babylon:

'I think there is so much strength in me that I shall overcome all things, all sufferings, even in order that I may say, and say with every breath: I am! I sit in the midst of a thousand torments—I am! I writhe in tortures—but I am! I sit in prison, but I live; I see the sun, or if I cannot see the sun, I know that it is. And to know that the sun is—that is the whole of life.'

Destroy this temple, and in three days I will raise it up. If I can't, my brothers will.